The Cambridge Psychological Library

PSYCHOLOGY
APPLIED TO EDUCATION

T0370547

PSYCHOLOGY
APPLIED TO EDUCATION

A SERIES OF LECTURES
ON THE THEORY & PRACTICE OF EDUCATION

by

THE LATE

JAMES WARD

SC.D. (CANTAB.), LL.D. (EDIN.), D.SC. (OXON.);
FELLOW OF THE BRITISH ACADEMY AND OF
THE NEW YORK ACADEMY OF SCIENCES;
PROFESSOR OF MENTAL PHILOSOPHY,
CAMBRIDGE

Edited by

G. DAWES HICKS

M.A., PH.D., LITT.D.
PROFESSOR OF PHILOSOPHY
IN UNIVERSITY COLLEGE
LONDON

Cambridge
at the University Press
1926

CAMBRIDGE
UNIVERSITY PRESS

University Printing House, Cambridge CB2 8BS, United Kingdom

Cambridge University Press is part of the University of Cambridge.

It furthers the University's mission by disseminating knowledge in the pursuit of education, learning and research at the highest international levels of excellence.

www.cambridge.org
Information on this title: www.cambridge.org/9781316603659

© Cambridge University Press 1926

First published 1926
First paperback edition 2016

A catalogue record for this publication is available from the British Library

ISBN 978-1-316-60365-9 Paperback

PREFACE

A few weeks before he died, on one winter's afternoon after we had been having a walk together, Professor Ward put the manuscript of these Lectures into my hands, asking that I should look through it and tell him whether I thought it contained anything that was worthy of publication. Several times previously he had spoken to me about his lectures on Education, saying that years ago they had cost him a considerable amount of labour, and that he had sometimes had the idea of revising them for the press. But he was always exceedingly dubious about the value of his own work, and he rarely committed anything to print without first of all seeking the judgment of his friends upon it, and requesting their criticism.

The Lectures appear to have been given originally during the Easter Term of 1880 in the Literary Schools at Cambridge, as a course arranged by the Teachers' Training Syndicate, and to have been re-delivered two or three times in succeeding years, once, I believe, in Newnham College. Since then, a great deal has been written both on the theory of Education in general and upon educational psychology in particular; and, had Professor Ward himself been preparing this book for publication, he would assuredly have referred to the more recent literature on the subject. But no one will doubt the propriety of giving to the Lectures as they stand a permanent form. Apart from the fact that the authorities whose names are mentioned and whose works are cited do not (except in the case of the last Lecture) belong to the present generation, there will be found in the volume little that is not as pertinent now as it was at the time when Dr Ward was writing. It is, in truth, surprising how completely the principles here propounded are in accord with the best that has been thought and said upon the theory of Education in recent years. Professor Ward had, I think, rather the impression that William James's *Talks to Teachers* had rendered his own Lectures superfluous. Yet, admirable as in many respects these *Talks* are, Dr Ward's treatment of the same problems is far more systematic, and should make the student of education realize the value of having a coherent and connected view of the growth and development of the mental life. Moreover, the Lectures are written in the author's happiest and brightest manner. They are enriched with a wealth of illustration which only a mind possessed as his was of an immense store of knowledge of nature and of human life could have summoned to the task; and they are replete with practical suggestions that can hardly fail to be helpful to teachers in whatsoever educational institutions they may be engaged. I believe, too, they will prove to be of value to the student of psychology. For they exhibit, in a striking way, how the leading ideas that are worked out in detail in the *Encyclopaedia* article on 'Psychology,' and which are more fully elaborated in the great treatise on *Psychological Principles*, give rise to and illuminate educational methods. I would refer especially, for example, to the extremely interesting discussion of Memory and of the relations of Language to Thought. Sometimes, indeed, it may not unfairly be claimed that the demands of a more popular presentation has led to a simpler and clearer statement of certain fundamental points, as, for instance, of the relation of pleasure to desire in Lecture IX.

Professor Ward's views on several psychological problems underwent modification with the lapse of years; and, in two or three instances, I have deemed it fitting to indicate by means of footnotes where such modification would have led him to alter the mode of treatment here followed. The most important case in point is in regard to the problems of Sense-Perception dealt with in Lecture IV, where I have ventured to add a Note at the end of the Lecture, explaining very briefly the analysis of the process which is to be found in detail in *Psychological Principles*.

Practically all the material comprised in the present volume was originally included in the series of lectures to which I have alluded. But Professor Ward made use of some portions of it for occasional Addresses which from time to time he was called upon to give, and where he did so I have availed myself of the later documents. This has entailed, now and again, some little amount of repetition; but it will not, I think, in any way interfere with the general course of the argument. Lecture XII on 'The Moral Education of the Young' was read as a paper to the London Ethical Society, though at what date does not appear; Lecture XIII on 'Individuality' formed the substance of an inaugural Address for the Session 1903–4 at University College, Aberystwyth; while the final Lecture on 'Personality' constituted the Presidential Address to the Civic and Moral Education League on 23rd May, 1917. The last mentioned was subsequently published in *The Hibbert Journal*; and Lecture VIII, on 'Education Values,' appeared as an article in the *Journal of Education*, for Nov. 1st, 1890. I have to acknowledge the courtesy of the proprietors of these periodicals for permission to re-publish the two Lectures named.

My sincere thanks are due to Professor W. R. Sorley and to Professor T. Percy Nunn, who have read through the proofs of this book, and helped me in preparing it for the press by a number of valuable suggestions.

G. DAWES HICKS

9 *August*, 1926

CONTENTS

Lecture I

THE POSSIBILITY AND VALUE OF A THEORY OF EDUCATION

Lecture II

THE GENERAL NATURE AND GROWTH OF MIND

Lecture III

GROWTH OF MIND (*cont.*): CHILDHOOD AND YOUTH

Lecture IV

PERCEPTION OF OBJECTS AND TRAINING TO OBSERVE

Contents

Lecture V

RETENTIVENESS, REPRODUCTION AND IMAGINATION

Lecture VI

THINKING, ABSTRACTION AND GENERALIZATION

Lecture VII

INTELLECTUAL AND LOGICAL TRAINING

Lecture VIII

EDUCATION VALUES

Lecture IX

DEVELOPMENT OF WILL AND FORMATION OF HABITS AND CHARACTER

Lecture X

VOLITION, SENSE OF JUSTICE, AND BENEVOLENCE

Lecture XI

DISCIPLINE AND AUTHORITY

Lecture XII

THE MORAL EDUCATION OF THE YOUNG

Lecture XIII

INDIVIDUALITY

Contents

Lecture XIV

PERSONALITY THE FINAL AIM OF EDUCATION

LECTURE I

THE POSSIBILITY AND VALUE OF A THEORY
OF EDUCATION

THE science of education is still in that stage of mixed being and non-being in which successful apology for its existence is requisite before it can really begin to exist. The value of treatises on the history and practice of education by educational experts is hardly likely to be questioned. But whether a student of psychology can contribute anything which it is worth a teacher's while to consider is a matter about which we may well be sceptical. And yet it is not hard to shew in a general way that a science of education is theoretically possible, and that such a science must be based on psychology and the cognate sciences. To shew this we have, indeed, only to consider that the educator works, or rather ought to work, upon a growing mind, with a definite purpose of attaining an end in view. For unless we maintain that the growth of mind follows no law; or, to put it otherwise, unless it be maintained that systematic observation of the growth of (say) a hundred minds would disclose no uniformities; and unless, further, it can be maintained that for the attainment of a definite end there are no definite means, we must allow that if the teacher knows what he wants to do there must be a scientific way of doing it. Not only so. We must allow not merely the possibility of a scientific exposition of the means the educator should employ to attain his end, but we must allow also the possibility of a scientific exposition of the end at which he ought to aim, unless again it be contended that it is impossible by reasoning to make manifest that one form of life and character is preferable to another.

What the laws of mind are we learn from psychology; in what this acquired perfection of man consists is largely the subject-matter of ethics. Thus the existence of a science of education appears to depend upon and follow from the existence of the so-called 'moral sciences,' among which psychology is the most fundamental. We find, accordingly, that on the Continent, where the aversion to theorizing is less pronounced than in this country, *Paedagogik*, as the Germans call it, is usually one of the subjects pertaining to a philosophic chair. All the leading philosophers of Germany have propounded theories of education; and among ourselves the names of Locke, James Mill, Whewell, Bain and Spencer at once occur as further instances.

But there are many, mostly somewhat stupid persons, who, instead of being helped by theory, are only mystified and cheated by the absence of such concrete and particular directions as they expected to find. To them the enthusiast who seeks to base education upon psychology is like Swift's tailor who took his customers' measure by means of astronomical instruments. There is no use measuring the man in such a philosophical fashion when after all a tape must be used to measure the cloth! What is the good of a knowledge of humanity in the abstract when you have to handle a room-full of restless little urchins?

No doubt a widespread distrust of educational theories has been produced by the extravagant claims advanced by the theorists themselves. Not to mention the unbounded pretensions of Ratich and Jacotot, Bell and Lancaster, we have in Rousseau and Pestalozzi examples of the mischief of indiscreet enthusiasm. The leading ideas of both these pioneers were as psychologically sound as they were practically important; but, being presented in too exaggerated terms, or overlaid with too much rose-colour, they have met with little but suspicion and neglect from English school-teachers.

Yet the question is worth asking whether, after all, the too sanguine expectations of so many educational reformers ought not to incline us rather to believe in than to reject the idea of a science of education. For where there is smoke, there is fire; where there is exaggeration, there is usually some truth. A man does not expect everything from a discovery from which he has already realized nothing of importance. Bacon and Descartes were most absurdly over-sanguine of the results that would follow the use of their methods; and even supposed that the supremacy of genius in the realm of science would disappear, much as mere physical superiority may be said to have disappeared from the modern battle-field after the invention of fire-arms. But, notwithstanding their unwarranted and unverified predictions, we none the less admit the first-rate importance of the methods of research expounded by the fathers of modern philosophy. And so we may admit that a science of education can never do the half of what educational theorizers have supposed, can never be comparable for exactness and distinctness to, say, the theory of navigation or the theory of structures; and yet have reason to believe that such a science will be as valuable to the practical teacher as the theories just mentioned are to the navigator and the engineer.

Dismissing as beneath contempt that 'platitudinizing formalism' which would affect to deduce from first principles the length of a school desk or a scholar's patience, quantities which experience only can enable us to estimate, we may none the less believe that the school-teacher's experience itself is only valuable to him, is only truly experience, when enlightened and interpreted by scientific theory. It would be well if those who eulogize experience as distinct from theory could be induced to give their minds to an examination of what they mean by this term 'experience.' The true antithesis is not, I venture to think, between theory or science on the one hand and experience or practice on the other, but between systematized and unsystematized experience, between experience that has been formulated and so made comprehensible and manageable and experience that remains blind and chaotic because it lacks both general ideas and unifying principles. The empirical knowledge of the so-called practical man is but raw material of the sort from which the man of theory elaborates the reasoned knowledge which we term science, the only knowledge which deserves to be called power, because the only knowledge which helps us to deal with new cases and to turn our concrete experiences to account. A knowledge, however intimate, of a narrow range of facts is worth very little, and the practical rules of thumb founded on such knowledge, though they may suffice for the attainment of a traditional standard, are worth very little too.

The history of the useful arts affords ample proof of this, so that even the City Companies are now looking to science to improve their wares. Yet, not only are the improvements in modern industry due to the substitution of scientific for empirical knowledge, but many of the advances in modern politics can be traced to the same cause. The world has still to learn how much it owes to political theorists like Adam Smith, Bentham or Montesquieu. The history of medicine furnishes, however, the aptest illustration for our purpose. It is some two thousand years ago now since medical men were divided, as perhaps educationalists are to-day, into the advocates and opponents of theory, or, as they were called, the rationalists and the empirics. The former asserted that, before attempting to treat any disease, we ought to make ourselves fully acquainted with the nature and functions of the body generally, with the operation of medical agents upon it, and with the changes which it undergoes when under the operation of any morbid cause; the empirics, on the contrary, contended that this knowledge is impossible of obtainment, and, if possible, is not necessary, that our sole guide must be experience, and that if we step beyond experience we are always liable to dangerous and often fatal errors. Of course, the rationalists knew nothing comparable with modern anatomy, physiology and pathology; but they believed in them afar off, and helped on their advent, while of their adversaries nothing remains but their name which is now synonymous with quack. Nobody supposes that a man is competent to practise medicine knowing nothing but anatomy, physiology and pathology; but nobody will maintain that he is competent, whatever may be his experience, if ignorant of these sciences. Similarly, no one, I imagine, supposes that a knowledge of psychology, logic and ethics, or rather of the science of education based on these, will suffice to make a man a school-teacher; but the day may come when, even in England, he who professes to be an educator without this knowledge will be esteemed little better than a charlatan and an empiric. And, if anyone should think this so much empty de-clamation, I would ask him to remember that the same would have been thought of a like prediction concerning medicine.

Nor will it appear too strong if we reflect for a moment longer on the superior practical worth of scientific or systematized know-ledge. *Vere scire est per causas scire*, said Bacon, and Aristotle before him had said the same thing; for, without this knowledge, we are almost as likely to attribute an effect to an unessential antecedent as to that which was really the cause of it, as, for example, the school-teacher does who attributes the improved memory of his pupils in after-years to the arduous gerund-grinding they had to do in their childhood, or their increased self-control to the disgust they had to overcome in doing it. And, conversely, till we know things through their causes we cannot foretell the effect of a given procedure nor turn our so-called experience to account: we are, indeed, more likely to add to the stock of prejudices and superstitions than to extend the range of useful knowledge. The man who, as a preliminary to practice, furnishes himself with a knowledge of theory may be compared to an agriculturalist who comes to his work with a stock of capital in the shape of time-and-labour-saving machinery. He grows richer every year, while his neighbour who has no tools but his own hands, *though he gets to work sooner*, makes no advance and dies as he began, a manual labourer. The man who turns aside to fashion a plough and harrow does not appear to be making such practical preparation for his food as the man who grubs up pig-nuts and takes his first meal on the spot; but the roundabout way secures the better dinner in the end. The man who studies psychology and the kindred sciences may appear to be taking anything but the directest way to proficiency as an educator, and yet, with the same stock of information, will far excel the 'hedge schoolmaster,' as Herbert Spencer called him, who has nothing but his mother-wit to aid him. Of course, the study of theory will not infallibly make any simpleton into a first-rate teacher, any more than gymnastics will convert a dwarf into a lifeguardsman. But out of a hundred teachers, fifty of whom have and fifty of whom have not made this preliminary study, we may, I think, safely affirm of the former three things: (i) that they will be on the whole the best teachers, (ii) that they will see most clearly wherein and why the current traditions of education are good or bad, (iii) that they will be most likely to improve existing theory and so to advance future practice.

Assuming, then, that a science of education is possible, and that if realized it would be of the greatest practical importance, not as superseding personal experience but as quickening and enlightening it, we may face the question: Are psychology and the related sciences at present sufficiently advanced to justify the attempt to deduce and formulate a system of educational principles? I should answer in the affirmative, and I hope in the course of these lectures to do something towards making my answer good. At the same time, I hasten at once to say that it is not my intention to attempt the construction of a theory of education. I do not at present feel competent to do this; and, even if I were, I should prefer to explain the elements of psychology on which such theory must largely rest. The teacher who has a fair knowledge of psychology can see the 'why' and 'wherefore' of any theory that is offered him, can even to a large extent make his own theory, or, at any rate, intelligently apply and, by and by, supplement out of his own experience the theory with which he starts. Still, although for my part I believe that, if teachers are to be trained at all, they should be trained thoroughly, I am compelled just now to a compromise; and, in consequence, shall treat only of those parts of psychology which bear most directly upon education. And I shall do this rather with the hope of giving you a sample which may induce you hereafter to make the bulk your own, than with any expectation that you will find yourselves much more fitted for your task if you should unhappily think the modicum I offer you enough for your need and too much for your liking.

At the outset, what are we to understand by education? This is a question we can hardly shirk. A man who should set out on a voyage without knowing whither he was going would probably go to the bottom before long, and he who should essay to build he knew not what would soon have his bricks tumbling about his ears. Yet there is no ideal of education so definite as 38° N. lat. 22° E. long., or as an architect's plan for a new church or hall, and still the worst of schoolmasters does not make shipwreck of all his pupils or ruin their lives. Neither probably does the most arrant quack kill all his patients. But in both cases pupils and patients may be only the worse for the treatment they received, and may have mended in spite of all, and thanks to a certain *vis medicatrix naturae*. We can, then, on no account assume that it is not worth while to trouble about defining the end and aim of education, because our definition can only be vague and general; nor suppose that all the harm a bad educator can inflict does not often result from ignorance of what education ought to be.

Professor Bain, in his work on education, rejects as too comprehensive both the definition given by the founders of the Prussian National System—"the harmonious and equable evolution of the human powers"—and that given by Mill—"the realization of human perfection"—and proposes instead "the work of the school." But surely this is little better than a logical see-saw. What is the work of the school? And, until we know what is the work of the other factor implied here, the work of the home, how are we to tell whether our means and methods of education are complete? Two halves do *not* make a whole. We must first have before us as clearly as we can the whole aim and intent of education before we can determine the respective functions of parents and school-teachers. Moreover, this is much more a question of application than a question for the pure theory of education.

Nobody will deny that such phrases as "the perfection of human nature," "the harmonious and equable evolution of the human powers," are extremely comprehensive. Still, if they comprehend the truth, it is surely better to try and think the matter out and make the meaning more exact than to take refuge in a phrase that is not really more definite—I mean the work of the schoolmaster—though its concreteness makes it seem so. To this procedure

Professor Bain only objects (*a*) because of its difficulty, and (*b*) because it may involve controversy. But surely these are not worthy grounds for declining an attempt important in itself and otherwise highly desirable. For my part, I do not even think the danger serious. No doubt, if you propose, like the Jesuits, so to instil the dogmas of some special sect or school that your pupils shall have neither the power nor the inclination to exercise their private judgment on these matters, or if, as in one place Professor Bain seems to do, you propose the advantage of society as the end to aim at in education, then, in either case, agreement will be impossible. If, however, you consider a man perfect in proportion as he is master of himself, loyal to truth, zealous for justice, conscious of his own finitude and filled with reverence in the presence of that Power inscrutable which is shaping all things towards some far-off, perfect whole; if you consider that he is perfect in proportion as with well-developed body and mind his interests are many-sided, while he is at once guided by sound common sense and animated by sympathy for all men and affection for his friends —then, surely, substantial agreement should be within reach as to the aim of education. If not, such terms as wisdom and reverence, truth and justice, freedom and decision, can have no fixed meaning; and when we talk of a man of clear judgment, fine sympathies, resolute purpose, and cultured tastes, we can only be uttering empty words. Such a supposition is, of course, sheer absurdity; and we might at once proceed with our endeavour to determine more precisely the true conception of the end of education.

Nevertheless, it may be well to look, for a moment, at the amount of agreement there is as to what is not perfection, what is not harmonious development. All, save perhaps very small schoolboys, agree that a mere athlete is not a perfect man; and all, without exception, that a prodigy of learning, male or female, without physical endurance or any sort of bodily dexterity is not perfect either. Nor do people now esteem knowledge without judgment and insight, mere erudition without brains; although at the time of the revival of learning this excessive regard for ponderous and encyclopædic lore was almost universal and is still much commoner among school-teachers than it should be. Intellect is, however, it must be allowed, a good deal worshipped even in these days; and rightly, for to it we owe in very large measure our knowledge and the advances which knowledge has enabled us to make. Material resources or brute strength go for little without intellect: as Liebig, if I mistake not, said, "an ounce of brains is worth a ton of apparatus." And this which is true of science is equally true of practical life. Yet, on reflection, we must own that intellectual ability, however great, is rather a means than an end; and history tells us of only too many instances in which the highest intellect has been a curse both to its possessor and to the world. And not merely so, but to accomplish anything remarkable, whether good or bad, intellectual power must be directed by fixed purpose. Very inferior talents, combined with decision and steadiness of purpose, continually turn out superior in the race of life. A strong will is, then, even more a desideratum than a strong intellect; and we in England, at all events, admire pre-eminent determination and tenacity of purpose even more than pre-eminent intellectual endowment. But resolution, constancy and self-control, with vigour of mind and body to boot, do not, as we have seen, constitute a man perfect: he may have all these and be a fiend. There must not only be a strong will but a good will. In fact, Kant has hardly expressed himself too emphatically in saying, "there is nothing in the world which can be termed absolutely and altogether good, *a good will alone excepted.*" And by 'good will' we should, of course, understand more than mere benevolence, a will which is determined, as Mr Thring in his excellent little book, *Education and the School*, would put it, by a right love and a right hate. And here first we come upon decided difference of opinion; but, from the point of view of educational theory, the difference is not really serious. What are the right things to love and seek, and what the right things to avoid and hate, are questions that different people will answer differently as soon as they descend to details; but with such details the theory of education is not concerned.

Moral excellence is, then, the first and paramount aim of secular education: to the power of self-rule, which alone will secure internal freedom, peace within a man, there must be added a living spirit of right and benevolence, and an earnest and hearty activity for some end worthy of human energies and of a human life. In subordination to the attainment of such moral excellence, and as a means to it, the educator will seek also so to exercise the bodily and mental powers of the young as to ensure a *maximum permanent efficiency*. *Permanent* efficiency, I say, and it is a point of such importance that I cannot forbear emphasizing it even now in passing, though I shall have to refer to it again and again. The fondness which parents and school-teachers so often display for precocious talent and the exigencies of examinations lead over and over again to the sacrifice of permanent efficiency to present effect. How to make your pupil shine now, is one problem, how to make him think and act for good purpose when a man is another and very different problem, and the psychological conditions of success in the two cases are very different too. It behoves us never to forget, what, indeed, no one would deliberately deny, that it is the second and not the first which is the problem of education. But these bodily and mental powers, whose efficiency for after-life education ought to be made as great as possible, are not a mere aggregate like the tools in a carpenter's bag or the drawings in his desk. In the case of the body the difference is evident to our senses. Though we call its several parts organs or instruments, we call them also members of one organism, that is to say, a whole whose parts are mutually dependent and adapted to consentient harmonious activity. And such harmonious activity or health we see almost universally both in nature around us and in the playgrounds of our boys' and girls' schools. The evils of excessive activity in one direction, with enforced inaction in others as a consequence, being so patent in the case of the body, serve thus to bring more vividly before us the equally great but less evident distortion due to inharmonious and unreasonable exercise of the powers of the mind. I have a dim recollection of a ghastly satire on our modern life, in which those who had neglected the use of any of their senses or limbs in this world appeared in the next without them. Thus many a poor cab driver was little more than a pair of eyes and arms attached to a stump which fitted into a hole on his box much as his whip does now. Yet mental abortions quite as monstrous as this are common enough even in this world. The man who puts down *Paradise Lost* asking what it was meant to prove, the man who cannot construct the common pump without the binomial theorem as scaffolding, the man who can tell a sardonyx from a cornelian but fails to grasp the distinction between οὐ and μη, or that between momentum and energy—all these are one-sided, inharmonious mental developments. To be, as it were, all reasoning, all imagination, or all observation, is to be mentally halt and maimed. And such one-sidedness defeats its own end quite as certainly in the mental organism as in the physical. Science is not independent of imagination, nor abstract reasoning independent of concrete observation; nor is a vivid and healthy fancy independent of sober facts.

To sum up, then. Taking education to mean the educing or drawing out of faculties and capacities, there is an education of some sort in the mere fact of life. In this way Nature began the education of our race before we ourselves made any conscious efforts to do so. But, restricting ourselves, as we have all along been doing, to the conscious efforts of adults to determine the after-life of the young, we may, I think, find much more meaning in Stein's definition than Professor Bain seems to find. Education *is* "the harmonious and equable evolution of the human powers by a method based on the nature of the mind, so that every power of the soul is unfolded, every crude principle of life stirred up and nourished, all one-sided culture avoided, and the impulses on which the strength and worth of men rest carefully attended to." This last expression is, no doubt, too weak. Moral vigour, moral worth, are the primary things; and next comes such exercise and culture of physical and mental resources, as shall render these through life as efficient as possible. And the *theory* of education is a systematic exposition of the methods by which this end is to be attained, an exposition mainly based on the sciences of physiology, psychology and ethics.

There is, however, another term often used interchangeably with the term education, though wholly different from it, to which we must turn for a moment. I mean the term instruction or information. It is essential to the educating or training process that the pupil should himself exert whatever faculty is being trained. There is thus an educating process possible for every faculty of body and of mind which can be perfected by practice; and, beyond such reflex actions as sneezing, winking, crying, and the like, there is probably no power, actual or possible, in the child that cannot be awakened and improved by appropriate training. But, whereas in education the pupil is pre-eminently active, under instruction, as distinct from training, his attitude is comparatively passive and receptive. To instruct or impart knowledge is an art depending mainly on logic and rhetoric; in giving information we seek to save the recipient the trouble of thinking so far as we can. And, to this end, what we have discovered in one order and by one method we impart in another. The object being to save the reader's or hearer's time and effort, we avoid the roundabout, tentative route of our original explanation and take the shortest cut to the result. In merely imparting knowledge we endeavour as well as we can to gauge the calibre of the recipient's mind and to break up what we have to teach into such morsels as it can take in. And, if we have gauged rightly and the recipient has been interested, we have added to his store of knowledge but not necessarily to his power of acquiring new knowledge for himself and others. Nay, there is no small danger, if we are sufficiently skilful at this art of mental foraging and cookery, that the said recipient may lose both the power and the inclination to improve his own mind in any other sense than to store it with such information as is brought within the grasp of his present means of ready comprehension. And this, alas! is all that a good many people mean by improving their own minds or the minds of others. Lord Avebury describes a species of ant— one which it would never do to send sluggards to, albeit its name is *Polyergus*. It has been fed and cared for by slave-ants of another species so long, that one of them, which he kept alone, shewed no signs of eating in the midst of plenty, and would certainly have been starved to death, had he not put in a slave, which at once fell to, washed and brushed the idler, and filled his mouth with food. Now, I am not sure that there are not some people in the world who bear some resemblance to this ant—diligent readers of science primers and literature manuals, who see nothing new and learn nothing fresh from all the wealth of Nature and Art, if left to themselves. For, in the application of his knowledge, and in the acquisition of knowledge which is above his present powers of comprehension, a man must use his wits; but in the mere reception of what he can now understand, there is very little more concerned than passive attention and memory.

But, granting that instruction may in certain cases and indirectly furnish some training to the mind, it is doubtful if it has even this collateral advantage when the matter of instruction is the nature of right conduct or virtue. If we distinguish teaching from training, we must say, I think, that virtue cannot be taught. To make your pupil virtuous, you must not preach to him, but lead him to practice. Virtue is a habit or disposition and habits can only be formed by repeated actions.

I am painfully aware how trite these remarks will seem; and yet, trite as they are, everywhere admitted in words, they are almost everywhere ignored in practice. Nine people out of ten, school-teachers included, act as if the end of education could be secured by the continual presentation and iteration of small doses of useful knowledge and excellent moral precepts. All the first-rate writers on education, from Locke onwards or even earlier, have insisted that the end of education can only be secured by training, and yet training is still lost sight of in the eagerness to impart information, to get over the ground, and fill the young mind with excellent moral precepts. The reason of a phenomenon so singular is worth inquiring into. One cause, I think, is haste to see tangible results. In the case of our primary schools, or Folkschools, as Mr Quick would have us call them, the problem of the school-teacher is no doubt very difficult. Certain proficiencies have to be acquired by a certain time as a means of livelihood, and the practical question is how far the impartation of useful knowledge can be made educative. And in the secondary schools, where a liberal education is intended, eagerness for success in examinations brings about much the same result. But the chief cause is perhaps ignorance, an ignorance which only a theory of education and the training of teachers will cure. Unfortunately, however, the evil tends to perpetuate itself; for it is largely because instruction and not training has been regarded as the main thing that this need of a remedy has not been felt. What a man knows he can teach to others, it is said. Possibly he can, although even this is by no means certain, if those others are adults like himself and interested in his subject. Yet he may have mastered his subject never so well and be unable to make it a means of mental training, if he knows nothing of the new and special conditions of this very different problem. Our stock of wise sayings would be without the one, "you cannot put old heads on young shoulders," if people did not try the foolish experiment a great deal too often. The fact is we soon forget that we were ever children, and probably, if we tried, we could not now recall the steps by which we have grown into our present selves. Hence the tendency, without reflection, to regard the child's mind and outlook as very much the same as our own; and, because it is instruction, not training, that *we* seek, instruction rather than training is what we think good for the young. Perhaps I put this a little too strongly. Still, it is, I believe, a fact that ignorance of psychology, or its application to the work of education, is the chief reason why training is so much sacrificed to instruction.

It is, then, by training, and not by mere instruction that the end of education is to be attained. We cannot, of course, train without instructing, but that knowledge which is the most useful in itself may be the most useful as a means of training. Herbert Spencer was of opinion that it is and must be so. "It would," he writes, "be utterly contrary to the beautiful economy of Nature, if one kind of culture were needed for the gaining of information and another kind were needed as a mental gymnastic[1]." But I do not think we can safely trust an *a priori* argument of this kind: Nature is often far too wasteful for that. Moreover, it is the business of reason to improve upon Nature's sure but roundabout processes. Leaving, however, for the present the question as to the 'education values' of different branches of knowledge, let us consider awhile the idea of training itself.

Training we may say is *directed growth*. To the pupil belongs the activity on which the growth depends, to the teacher the ideal or end by which the growth is directed and the methods of bringing this direction to bear on the pupil's activity. It is in this sense that the term is used in the familiar case of training trees and shrubs: the gardener cannot train his tree while yet a seed, he must wait till its branches begin to shoot; nor can he train the seedling in the winter when it has temporarily ceased to grow nor after it has reached maturity and ceased to grow altogether. Education is possible when growth begins and so long as there is growth; although education by another need not, and, indeed, cannot, last so long, for so far as the pupil consciously adopts an ideal for his own life so far he begins to educate himself and assumes an independence incompatible with determination by some other person. But this by the way. The point now to be insisted upon is that the continuous activity of the faculty to be trained is the *conditio sine quâ non* of training. We see this fairly well in what are not very accurately termed bodily exercises. There is but one way to learn drill and that is to go through the movements: the private cannot put off the sergeant with a description of how the sergeant performed them, while he stood at ease himself. Nor could a teacher be very easily imposed upon either, if he were not already to some extent imposed upon by the general practice of accepting repetition, by rote and rule, of his own observations and inferences in place of directing the spontaneous efforts of his pupils to see and think for themselves. Then, however, comes the objection that this process, besides being more difficult for the teacher, is so slow; and this very true remark leads to another point, that growth is slow, slow it seems to us who look only at the result, but not slow when we consider how many steps that we have never known or have forgotten such growth entails. It is a sad moment in the life of a boy, who has perhaps been wisely educated at home, when

[1] *Education: Intellectual, Moral and Physical*, chapter i, cheap ed., p. 41.

he allows himself to substitute memory for mastery, in order to keep pace with a school which is forced on by examinations. It is still sadder, though happily now much rarer, when he is led to play the moral prig, under the stress of a parental solicitude, ignorant that the natural time for heart-searchings and self-scrutiny is not yet.

And this carries us naturally to the further remark, that, since training depends on the spontaneous activity of the pupil, it becomes all-important to ascertain the order in which the several faculties to be trained manifest themselves. Under the old instruction régime, this was a question practically ignored; and, in consequence, the natural order was almost as much violated as it could be. It was impossible, of course, to teach algebra before arithmetic, for example; but, within the limits of each subject, the method pursued was the method of exposition, not the method of acquisition. And still worse, because knowledge was the main thing, the memory was at once loaded with as much as it could carry of material that could not possibly be assimilated for years to come, as if memory were a kind of mental cud, independent of the mind as a whole, in which, therefore, food for future rumination could be advantageously stored up!

Both these points, then—i.e. the laws of mental growth and the order in which the several faculties develop—must occupy us at length hereafter.

There remains, however, at all events, one inquiry of an introductory character to which we may now turn—namely, what are the conditions of effectively *directing* growth? Passing by the obvious one that we must begin early, that is to say, when mental pliability or plasticity is at a maximum, so that the first advance shall be right and no after-energy wasted in correcting early faults, the first condition of success is to secure *interest*. By interest I mean, of course, direct and spontaneous interest, not that wasteful and reflected interest which is based upon the pressure of external compulsion, where the pupil is forced to do what is distasteful to avoid what is more distasteful still. "One volunteer is worth ten pressed men" is by no means the weakest argument against the use of the now obsolete impressment laws; and the like is true, and for a like reason, of school. What the scholar does because he likes to do is worth ten times as much as anything which he is forced to do when he dislikes it. And no wonder, since, in the one case, all his energies are engaged in the most efficient way, i.e. voluntarily;

and have besides their efficiency still further increased by the additional vitality and zest due to pleasurable occupation. Whereas, in the other case, fear and dislike repress a large part of his energies; and, of what is available, a further portion still has to be engaged in forcibly keeping up attention to the task in hand and restraining the momentary distractions due to the disturbing ideas that will intrude where absorption is not spontaneous and complete. Astonishment is continually expressed at the extraordinary acquisitions of self-educated men, whereupon the result is at once put down to genius and everybody is satisfied. Yet genius is here only a name for a number of co-operating causes, and, among these, interest is one of the chief. If genius is to mean only unwonted facility, self-educated men are, by no means, always men of genius. The trouble they take is enormous. The secret of their success is not always or wholly or chiefly extraordinary ability but extraordinary interest. Their whole soul is in their work, no power is wasted while they are at it, though much is misspent for want of guidance. Every teacher allows that it is better to secure the interest of his pupil or class; and those who have the tact to do so rank as good teachers. But the vital importance of this point, so far as I can make out, is very far from being recognized. When direct spontaneous interest is not forthcoming, there is still the other way of enforced attention and performance; and, after all, it always has been necessary to resort to this, and, accordingly, it is resorted to again. And so parents, pupils and teachers alike acquiesce in it as inevitable; this they do the more readily because of a widespread superstition that there is virtue in pain, what Herbert Spencer calls "the greatest-misery principle[1]." It is true that self-restraint is one of the habits education has to induce; but to this end it is not desirable to multiply the means of mortification, any more than it is desirable to have dear bread to teach people economy. If lessons could be pleasant and interesting from the beginning of school-life to the close of it, it would be a most enormous gain. It would be like sailing for ever before a wind, instead of continually lying to or bearing up slowly helped by a mere fraction of a strong but contrary breeze.

It would really be worth while to impress upon oneself the difference between interesting and uninteresting occupation in some definite way. Bore yourself for two or three hours by studying a book on the dullest subject you know of—say, a German treatise

---

[1] *Op. cit.* p. 50.

on Gnosticism or Mr Casaubon's *Key to all the Mythologies*—and then give as much time to some book with which you have long been anxious to make acquaintance, such as *The Life of Gordon*. Note your feelings while reading in each case, and recall what you have learnt in the two cases a week or so after; and then reflect for a while on the unhappy lot and the wasted energies of a child whose delight is Hans Andersen or Grimm's goblins, or the rearing of silkworms and the capture of butterflies, or the fashioning of a wooden windmill or a water-clock, but who is provided with no occupation more congenial to his tastes than strings of dates, endless paradigms and bills of parcels or tare and tret. I do not say all work can be as pleasant as play, but the greater part of it can be made interesting, though to do this will be difficult. Yet, if the value of interest were sufficiently realized, more efforts would be made to surmount the difficulty.

LECTURE II

THE GENERAL NATURE AND GROWTH OF MIND

Before proceeding to the subject of the present lecture I wish to say a word upon physical education. I cannot at all agree with Professor Bain that this is a matter which lies outside the province of educational theory. A comparatively independent branch of such theory no doubt it is, although acquaintance with the conditions of bodily health would be a matter of no small importance, even were intellectual training our only concern. But for parents, private tutors, and the heads of school-houses, knowledge of how to promote the physical growth and vigour of the young is indispensable. Too many continental writers on education have followed Professor Bain in ignoring the claims of the body and its intimate connexion with the mind. And the result is that, while their class work and discipline are admirable, it has lately been found that in some schools a third of the scholars suffer from headaches, due mainly to long school-hours and too much home preparation, which has to be done chiefly, of course, at nights. Not a little harm has, I suspect, been caused by the over-statement we often hear, "change of work is as good as play." It is no such thing. Good no doubt it is, and better than entire idleness in many cases, but play is work for children, that is to say, it is active occupation; and change to this form of work they require at pretty frequent intervals, if their other work is to have any zest in it. A healthy child three years old runs perhaps two or three miles in the course of the day, but would be seriously tired if it had to run a quarter of a mile at once. Children are soon exhausted and soon refreshed. And we have to remember that their brains, like the rest of their bodies, have a double work to do where the work of the adult brain is only single; the child's brain has both to act and to grow. Nay, it has to grow in two respects, both necessitating frequent relaxation or entailing certain injury. It has to grow in bulk and it has to grow in complexity of structure. Beside sufficient but not excessive exercise, the chief condition of growth in bulk is well-nourished and well-aerated blood; and with this condition long confinement is incompatible. The chief condition of the other and higher growth is due to rest after exercise to enable the new nervous connexions to perfect themselves. The brain is not a delicate organ in the sense of being easily hurt by work, and even hard work; but it is extremely delicate in this sense, that all forcing and excessive strain deteriorate it in strength and still more perhaps in quality; it is, in this respect, like a good watch which will serve you your life-time with care, but is almost sure to snap somewhere if you overwind it. Parents and headmasters and mistresses must have a real acquaintance, though it need not be profound, with the physiological laws on which bodily growth and vigour depend before the rising generation can be secure against "the educational abomination of desolation," as Professor Huxley calls it, that brain-forcing which is now too much in vogue in secondary schools. Without this, the foolish public is just as likely, if it should ever become alarmed, to err to an equal extent in the opposite extreme and refuse to children the mental quickening their brains require.

But, besides these, there is a much more intimate connexion than is commonly supposed between moral health and bodily health. I do not mean that soundness of body is alone sufficient to ensure generosity and purity of heart, but that active exercise is a check to many temptations which are only too powerfully abetted by sluggish limbs and hysterical nerves, while "he whom toil has braced or manly play" has not only "light as air each limb, each thought as clear as day," but most likely has too an abounding good nature and cheerfulness which provoke and strengthen friendly feeling. For my own part, the more I think about it the more I am persuaded that a course of lectures on the elements of physiology applied to education is as much needed as a course like the present.

Turning, then, now, to the proper subject of this lecture, our first business must be to get some general notion of what we mean by the mind. For a long time it has been the custom to represent the mind as a complex of faculties,—faculties of sense, of memory, of imagination, of judgment, of reasoning, of emotion, of volition, and so forth *ad indefinitum*. But this terminology, though it has its conveniences, and is besides one we can hardly discard in ordinary conversation, has nevertheless been the occasion of frequent errors and will lead us also astray, if we do not make clear to ourselves what we understand by it. In the body we know there are definite organs, having definite functions,—the heart to propel the blood, the liver to purify it, the lungs to oxygenate it, and so forth. And, when careful and long-continued observation had disclosed the fact that in the brain we have an organ holding a most intimate relation to the mind, so that for example a well-developed and well-nourished brain was concomitant with excellence and vigour of mind, or intoxication or disease of the brain with delirium or aberration of mind, then, on the strength of this fact and in conformity with the faculty theory, it was confidently and reasonably concluded that within the brain itself would be found in one part the organ of memory, in another the organ of imagination, in another the organ of volition, and so on. Time would fail me to tell of all the attempts, extending over half a century, to find organs for supposed faculties and faculties for supposed organs. Meanwhile, the opinion has steadily gained ground that the so-called faculties are but psychological abstractions, names due at first to a faulty classification of facts, the real explanation of which they served at length to hide. To the question, how does a man move about? I answer, rightly, by means of his legs. But to the question, how does he remember? there is only the semblance of information in the answer: By means of his memory. Legs are a reality, and only one among several possible instruments of locomotion: fish swim and birds fly. Yet memory is not in this sense a reality, as will be apparent directly from a parallel case. Professor Huxley, it is said, is a masterly expositor of science. How does he expound science so ably? By means of his admirable faculty for exposition. It is clear that there is here no advance. What is the moral? Let us see what the physicists did in a similar perplexity. A needle moves towards a magnet placed near it, or the needle is dissolved in sulphuric acid. How? Owing to the magnetism of the magnet and the solubility of the needle was the sort of explanation first offered and accepted,—an explanation which carries us no further than giving a name to the phenomena or actions to be explained. And during this stage everything was regarded as the seat of, or as endowed with, a multiplicity of powers and properties by which its actions and reactions were supposed to be determined. But the explanation which the physicist now gives, or seeks to give, consists in shewing what was the arrangement of the body concerned (i) at the beginning, (ii) at the end, of the action in question, and (iii) the quantity of energy it has lost or gained in the passage from the one arrangement to the other—facts, that is, which can in all cases be represented by a certain configuration in space and by reference to some given quantity of matter moving through a given distance in a given time. The unity of the physical world was in danger of being lost sight of amid the multitude of forces and powers: the unity of mind is still in similar danger. Can we, to avoid this, substitute for the reference to a host of faculties, current in the old psychology, any conceptions as definite as matter and motion, so as really to explain the facts only named before? It would be too bold to say 'yes' and I do not like saying 'no.'

Look for a moment at what has befallen the phrenologists. The progress of physiology has at length placed it beyond reasonable doubt that there are no organs in the brain at all having any sort of analogy with mental faculties   In the brain and its continuation, the spinal cord, we have millions of microscopic cells which are the terminations of nerve fibres, coming from all parts of the body, and other cells again forming centres for a network of connexions between those first cells, and connected again in turn in like manner with cells higher still, and so on. The nerves reaching the brain and spinal cord from the rest of the body are of two kinds, and two kinds only; those which start from moving or active parts like muscles and those which start from sensitive parts like the skin, the eye or the ear. Under normal circumstances, the latter nerves are stimulated or set into action by some change produced by the external world on the sensitive surface in which they terminate— say of the tips of the fingers, or the retina of the eye. The effect of this change then travels up the nerve to the brain: hence these are called centripetal or ingoing nerves. Under normal circum- stances, again, the other kind of nerve is stimulated by a change taking place in the brain cells. The effect of this change travels down the nerve, and, by exciting the muscle to move, produces some change in the external world: hence these are called centri- fugal or outgoing nerves. The cell in which an ingoing nerve terminates is connected with some cell in which an outgoing nerve begins, so that the excitation which reaches the first passes on and arouses the second; and thus the action of the external world on the body is followed by a reaction of the body upon the external world. When one bird hops on to a trap, the trap reacts, and the bird is caught: when another hops into a crocodile's mouth, the mouth closes and he is caught too: what springs and wires accom- plished in the one case, nerves, nerve-cells and muscles accom- plish in the other. And, as by a more elaborate contrivance of springs and wires a more elaborate trap could be produced, so, by a more complicated connexion between nerve-cells or centres, more elaborate reactions to the actions of the external world become possible. This, then, is all that physiology certainly finds in a brain: neither more nor less than a vastly complex mechanism of exceeding delicacy, whose function it is to co-ordinate and adapt the reactions of the body to the actions of the external world, a mechanism which is more complex (i) the more ways there are in which the external world can affect the body, (ii) the more ways there are in which the body can react by moving, and (iii) the more ways there are in which possible actions and reactions may be combined. Thus, by way of illustration, an animal that has eyes and ears has a more complex brain than one that has eyes only; an animal that has both arms and legs than one that has arms only; an animal that moves either arms or legs after the stimulation of either eyes or ears than one that can only move its legs when its ears are stimulated and its arms when its eyes are. Concomitantly with the brain-changes described, there are certain mind-changes: to centripetal stimulations correspond sensations, hence the centripetal nerves and their cells are often, though not accurately, called *sensory*; to centrifugal stimulations correspond the exertion of movement, for which reason these nerves and their cells are called *motor*. When definite portions of the brain are destroyed by injury or disease, hearing ceases, though the ear and its nerves remain intact; when other definite portions are destroyed, sight ceases. With the destruction of other parts, again, the power to move the right hand is lost, of yet other portions the power to move the left, and so on. Further, the loss of particular parts renders particular co-ordinated movements, such as walking or articulation, impossible. And so, part by part, the whole brain, anatomically regarded, furnishes us with equivalents to nothing in mind but sensations and movements, and complexes of sensations and movements.

And, now, instead of studying others' brains, for we cannot see our own, let us turn to our own minds, which none but ourselves can see. What have we here? Nothing but sensations and movements or complexes of these, the physical equivalents of which we find to constitute the whole structure of brain? Nothing, I believe, except the mind which is conscious of having all these, together with the pleasure or pain it receives from them. I do not expect you at once to accede to this: I hope, nevertheless, to do something to make good my analysis as we go along. But the first thing is to get it into better shape. Prior even to this, however, I want to digress for a moment to obviate an objection that may occur to someone—an objection with which I entirely sympathize. You may say with not unnatural aversion: Are, then, our noblest thoughts and aspirations nothing but complexes of sensations and movements, the concomitants in some mysterious way of material changes in the brain? No, the reality of your thoughts and emotions—so far as reality stands for meaning and worth—lies in these as they are when you think them and feel them, just as the reality of Nature lies in the living form and face of Nature, not in the decompositions, whether logical or material, which aid our curiosity when we try to know not *it* but *about* it. A chill disappointment is sure to seize us if we imagine that the reality is what we have reached by our analysis and dissection, instead of being what we have left behind. We seek to know about the parts of Nature that we may the better appreciate and understand the whole. In this spirit, then, let us resume our analysis of mind.

The simplest state of mind we need consider at the outset would be some such as the following: There comes before you the perfume of a rose; you are pleased and either stoop to enjoy it more or you pluck the rose. Here then are (i) an object presented and attended to, (ii) the feeling it produces in you, the subject attending to it, and (iii) the action which follows upon the pleasure. But, here, note that this action is only possible by attending to it while you do it. There are here, then, two sorts of things attended to; and in this case, at all events, they are not obviously different from sensations and movements. Suppose, however, you have just read the scene in *King John* where his nephew is to have his eyes put out. Here there is strictly speaking no sensation, but the scene as you picture it is made up of what still remains of past sensations, and if you had had the misfortune to have been born blind much of the scene would be unmeaning. Neither is there here, perhaps, any movement, unless your feeling of pain at the horrible scene should find vent in words or facial expression. Yet, at any rate, there are the beginnings of movements, as you imagine yourself raising an alarm, or attempting a rescue. Or, suppose you reflect awhile on the saying: "Virtue is its own reward." Such a state of mind is enormously complex, as you will at once realize if you imagine yourself expounding the maxim to a boy of twelve. Virtue stands for virtuous acts, or for a life of such, and this has finally to be pictured out in detail by means of what the boy has himself seen and done in the past. It would be tedious to multiply illustration further. Try, if you choose, for yourselves and see if you do not find that the material of all that can be presented to our minds is reducible to sensations and movements, just as the material of all the vast variety of substances on the earth is reducible to some one or more of the chemical elements.

The greatest part of our work is, it is clear, in both cases, to study the compounds. The inquiry of chief interest in psychology is, then, that concerning the formation of complex ideas out of simple ones, of perceptions out of sensations, of thoughts out of perceptions. It is easy to take to pieces, but putting together again is a very different matter. Locke, who was very successful at the first process, the analysis, failed completely at the second, the synthesis. Let us, then, take care, and advance only a step at a time.

First, what is requisite in order that two or more sensations and movements should form a complex? There is no sort of psychical cement or psychical attraction, so far as we know, or can at present conceive. The one condition for forming a psychical compound is contiguity. This is why when hearing the voice of a friend there is at once present to our mind his appearance as well. But this connexion is not as close as it might be, because it is sometimes broken. We hear our friend's voice without seeing him, or see him when he does not speak. On the other hand, some of the complexes formed never have their elements in this way presented apart, or, if presented apart at first, become after a time so closely conjoined that we cannot by introspection separate them. In these cases the complexity only admits, of course, of indirect proof and the fact of it is apt to be overlooked. Most persons, for example, would regard the sight of a coloured surface as an elementary fact, since we see no uncoloured surface and no non-extended colour. This is one source of the inability of adults to understand the difficulties children have in apprehending what to their teachers seems absolutely simple and self-evident.

Next, let us ask in what ways the needful contiguity is brought about. For the present, we need only to note two which are of fundamental importance. In many cases, sensations are presented to us over and over again grouped in the same way. Thus, we have the whiteness, softness and coldness of snow; the colour, taste and fragrance of an orange; the brightness and warmth of a fire, and so on. In this way, groups or complexes of sensations are formed, independently of the mind or subject to whom the sensations belong, independently, that is, so far as the character of the group is concerned. But in the case of movement it is to a large extent otherwise. When sensations occasion us pleasure, we move either to express our pleasure or to secure its continuance; when sensations occasion us pain, we make movements expressive of pain or on purpose to be rid of it. Such movements, being contiguous with the sensations, become associated with those sensations and will together give rise to a new and more complex state of mind. Thus, to repeat my former instance, the perfume of a rose leads to the act of plucking it, the means whereby the scent of many former roses was more fully enjoyed. Similarly, the dog that has been thrashed cowers or runs away at the sight of the whip, from the smart of which his legs or his humble demeanour delivered him before. These, then, are the two sources by which the material of our experience is brought together and formed into complexes or united wholes: first, independently of us, the external world, and secondly, independently of the external world, ourselves, i.e. our interest in our own feelings of pleasure and pain, which determine our movements or reactions to it.

Owing to a certain constancy in these two factors, complexes originally formed are united for the most part more closely by repetition. Day after day, we have presented to us together the same arrangements of the world about us; day after day, the same pleasures and pains lead to the same movements to secure or avoid the causes of them. And, thus, out of what is originally much such a chaos as the world resolved into its chemical elements would be there arises, by this process of combination and re-combination, what we call our experience, the contents of our mind. It is by carefully following this process as it advances to more and more complex forms that we must hope to obtain real explanations of those mental phenomena to which the theory of faculties does but give names. This, of course, we cannot attempt, except in a few cases, within the limits of these lectures.

But now let me briefly summarize, and, in one or two points, supplement this meagre sketch of the general nature of mind. We have in what we call mind (i) a subject or self, whether it knows itself or not, which is conscious of objects or ideas and (ii) the ideas or objects of which it is conscious, using the terms idea and object in a very wide sense. Such mental objects[1] in their simplest,

---

[1] [In his later writings, particularly in his *Psychological Principles* (1918), Professor Ward recognized that such terms as 'mental object' and 'mind-object' are calculated to mislead. In these later writings, he very definitely repudiated the view that sensations are to be regarded as 'states of consciousness,' or 'subjective

crudest, form are (*a*) sensory objects or (*b*) motor objects, or, in more familiar language, sensations and movements. We can only be definitely conscious of, that is to say, attend to, a few of these at a time. Those to which we attend together, whether sensory or motor objects, or partly the one and partly the other, thereby tend to form a new whole or *complex* idea. And, when other objects succeed to the first place in our attention—the place which is usually either given to or seized by new comers—this complex idea or mind-object[1] does not dissolve and disappear utterly, like a "snowflake on a river." It is only crowded out into a dim or dark background, which we may call the region of subconsciousness, that is to say, the region of all but unconsciousness. From this region, it can again emerge, not resolved into its components, but the same complex object as before, though fainter in intensity, and, so far, securing less attention. Once more in the forefront of consciousness its elements are more closely combined; moreover, at any time when thus revived it may enter into the composition of another object of consciousness more complex still; and so, step by step, the mind is said to grow.

We may, now, perhaps, proceed to consider this growth in more detail. The actual beginning of consciousness is as indescribable as the beginning of life. Even the earlier stages of consciousness can only be inferred from a study of the later by interpreting the external behaviour of infancy in analogy with the external behaviour of the later stages. But, among the materials of consciousness, the sensory and motor objects

modifications, either affective or active.' If they were affective states of the subject, they would, he pointed out, be feelings, which they assuredly are not; and, although they certainly imply the conscious activity of attention, it is not, he urged, as modifications or states of this activity, but as objects of it, that they imply it. He used the term 'presentations' in a comprehensive way to embrace "sensations, movements, percepts, images, intuitions, concepts, notions"; and what Locke said of 'ideas' he would say of 'presentations,'—namely, that they are "the immediate objects of our minds in thinking." Like Locke also, he distinguished between *these* objects and what are commonly called 'physical' objects, objects conceived as independent of any particular subject. But the psychologist, he maintained, is concerned with objects as they are presented to experiencing individuals, as they are apprehended by conscious minds. And, as thus regarded, an object is, no doubt, partially dependent, so far as its nature is concerned, upon the mind that apprehends it; it is, in short, the way in which the real entity (or real 'object') appears to this or that knowing subject; and appearances of the same real entity will vary for different individuals and, at different times, for the same individual. This, however, does not mean that the appearances, the presentations, are 'states of consciousness' or 'subjective modifications.' Appearances can only be said to be 'in consciousness' in the sense that they are presented *to* consciousness.—*Ed.*]

[1] *Ibid.*

presented to the young soul, when attention first awakens, we may safely reckon all the varieties of sights, sounds, touches, tastes, smells, for which it has organs and opportunities and all the movements its limbs by any chance may execute. We may go further, and, instead of supposing the entire formation of this mental chaos into a mental cosmos to depend on the child's own activity, may reasonably suppose that it starts with certain lines of association, at least, prepared beforehand and vaguely indicated. To grant this is to grant the doctrine of psychical heredity, the doctrine, that is, that those connexions which were slowly established between some cells and others in the brains of its ancestors in the course of, and in consequence of, their experience, are already more or less completely preformed in the child's brain before its experience begins—so far preformed that a minimum of experience, in its case, suffices to perfect the connexion, say, between a certain sensation and a certain movement, which in the case of its forefathers was only perfected after the lapse of years, perhaps of centuries. It is to this inherited difference of organization, and consequent difference of mental possibilities, that we must often refer the varying rapidity with which different minds unfold in particular directions, and the varying interest they take in different pursuits.

In view of facts like these—which I regret I cannot here consider more fully—one may be pardoned for doubting whether the same means will be equally adapted in all cases to secure the same end: whether what will best train one mind and disposition will best train another and different mind and disposition. People in the western counties travel eastwards to get to London, but those in the eastern counties would have an expensive and fatiguing journey if they did the same. It is not, then, enough for parents and teachers to have distinctly before them an educational ideal; it is hardly less important that they should understand the individuality, as we say, of their pupils. Even a horsebreaker cannot dispense with such knowledge: much more is it impossible to be a good educator without the tact and insight to understand one's pupils. This perhaps is one of the points as to which it is true that a good teacher is born not made. How few there are in any community who can enter into many lives besides their own, enjoy seeing others ride hobbies they would never mount themselves: broad in their tastes and broader still in their sympathies, to whom everybody tells his good news and not a few confess

their faults or bring their difficulties! These are the men and
women, when you can find them, to choose for schoolmasters and
schoolmistresses. But there is much truth in the old rhyme:
"Evil is wrought by want of thought as well as want of heart."
No institutions are so conservative as educational institutions—
a fact for which it is not hard to find reasons. After the
revival of learning the idea of training had dawned on but two
or three minds, and the circle of useful knowledge was so small
that it was natural to set all alike to tread the same weary
round. And so the tradition has become established which is
continually treating minds the most diverse after the same anti-
quated fashion. To many teachers, I daresay, it never occurs to ask
what *intellectual* training will be best for this pupil and for that: so
far as moral training goes, that must, indeed, be a very perfunctory
and clumsy teacher who treats all alike. No doubt it requires
some experience to make the most of clever but odd children, and
the practical difficulties must often be considerable. Still, spite of
all, in discussing the theory of education we ought to take account
of the mischief done by trying to poll all the minds in a school
to one shape just as the country barber polls their hair. If anyone
should doubt that the mischief is great let him read the results of
an inquiry on this point made by Sir Francis Galton and tabulated
in his *English Men of Science, their Nature and Nurture*.

But it is primarily with what is common to the growth of all
minds that we have now to do and here also there is room for some
weighty practical reflections. Let us, however, first see something of
the growth itself. Though the organized experience of its ancestors
may enormously accelerate the infant's earliest progress in knowledge, yet we shall not be far wrong in supposing it to advance
by gradual steps even here. Its great defect at the outset is inability to concentrate attention. For want of this, it is some time
before even the first step can be taken towards the simplest combination of the material constantly provided for it by its senses
and its own spontaneous or instinctive movements. The 'massive'
sensations of organic life, the sensations and movements connected
with breathing, pulses, digestion, the feeling of being well or ill—
to all of which we adults are oblivious, except when they are very
pronounced, because our interests carry our attention elsewhere—
these organic sensations probably form for some time the staple
elements of the infant consciousness. Amid such a mass, the light
and transient impressions of the higher senses fail at first to afford

any pleasure, and so fail to call forth any interest, comparable to the solid satisfaction of a vigorous digestion and a glowing pulse: the young hopeful vegetates triumphantly. After a while, however, the preliminaries and essentials of a meal come, by reason of their contiguity in time to the meal itself, to secure some attention and to be known by themselves: to the spoon belongs the merit of first enticing the baby mind into the regions of objective knowledge. Soon the fortunate moments become more and more frequent in which a moving light, the jingle of a rattle, or the magic pinches which nurses administer carry it still further in the same direction. Its consciousness is no longer that of a large oyster in a heavenly dream; the chaos before it begins to shape itself into nebulous wholes, faces and moving objects stand out vaguely from the general blur, and everybody is agreed that baby "begins to notice[1]." But how very obscure and ill-defined these earliest complexes or perceptions are is brought home to us most strikingly by comparing infantile movements with our own. There is no reason to suppose that the ability to perform any definite movements lags far behind the ability to form definite perceptions. A baby expresses his pleasure by the most various antics, in the course of which many movements that will afterwards be purposive occur by chance; but it is long before any one can be performed apart from the rest. The child at first can do nothing without doing

---

[1] ["Psychologists," it is remarked in *Psychological Principles* (p. 75), "have usually represented mental advance as consisting fundamentally in the combination and re-combination of various elementary units, the so-called sensations and primitive movements." By no writer was this notion of 'mental chemistry' more effectively disposed of than by Professor Ward. He shewed it to be an error to take for granted that the phases of experience which are the less developed, and which, on that account, may be described as the more simple, exhibit a simplicity of ultimate elements which, as evolution proceeds, merely enter into more and more complicated combinations. "The process," he pointed out, "seems much more like a segmentation of what is originally continuous than an aggregation of elements at first independent and distinct." What characterizes the earlier stages of experience is specially the want of definitiveness and of precision in the apprehension of relations among the contents discriminated. And the contents themselves appear as vague and obscure, wanting in sharpness of outline and loosely connected with one another. Objects are apprehended by a mental life containing but small preparation for the apprehension of them. Consequently, the awareness of them is crude and confused, and the confusion is aggravated by the circumstance that no steady background of 'self' has yet been formed, against which the successively apprehended contents can stand out in relief, as it were. The general mode of progress is, then, always from the indefinite to the relatively definite, from the indistinct to the relatively distinct, from the confused to the relatively clear. Experience, that is to say, does not start with the recognition of isolated, separate presentations; it is for psychology a problem to solve how gradually the recognition of isolated, separate sense-data, as they are now called, becomes possible.—*Ed.*]

everything. As the physiologists would put it, there is too much radiation and too little restriction. Every excitation arouses the whole brain instead of discharging itself along definite tracks, like a downpour of rain on some land new risen from the bed of the sea and on which the weather has still to trace out a network of streams and rivers. As the one process takes time, so does the other, though both seem very much matters of course to the unreflecting observer, when the development is complete.

Now, the great means of advancing this parcelling out of experience into parts, of making groups of definite objects and acts out of an indefinite maze of sensations and movements, or to use Herbert Spencer's favourite phrase, of progressing from the homogeneous to the heterogeneous, is *Interest*. The uniformity of Nature—the regular recurrence of sweet and white in sugar, of meows and scratches when puss is picked up by the tail—does much to suggest which two and two to put together. But ages may elapse before we take the hint, unless as in the above instances we are interested. And, for my own part, I doubt not that ages did elapse before the creature mind appreciated and appropriated even the most elementary lessons which an infinite patience had planned for it. Would that those who carry on Nature's work had more of Nature's patience!

Interest in sensations it is, as we have seen, that determines movements, and on movements in connexion with sensations a very large part of our knowledge depends. What we learn by means of our eyes and our hands would be reduced almost to *nil* if we were prevented from moving them. Interest also works by concentrating attention upon some objects to the exclusion of others. And here, again, its connexion with movement is apparent, though this time it is by checking movements that are begun, the continuance of which would draw off attention. In these two ways the infant individualizes objects, and separates, among the mass that is presented to it together, those things that belong together. The bucket that lies on the floor is distinguished from the floor on which it lies, and the clatter of a rattle from the many other sounds heard simultaneously. But, beyond this narrow region of its experience, or rather these isolated patches, into which its formative activity has introduced the beginnings of order, the primal indistinctness and confusion reigns, and will reign, till interest furnishes the budding intelligence with a motive to enter and assimilate.

This interest is, as we have seen, determined by pleasure and pain. But what determines these; what is there common to all that pleases us? If I answer *doing what we please*, it may perhaps be thought that this is as good as no answer at all. Yet it is much truer than at first sight it seems, that all pleasure involves doing, involves activity. Even the apparently passive pleasure of watching a display of fireworks or hearing the waves break upon the stones requires activity and involves fatigue; so that, if your eyes or ears were already exhausted or you were yourself generally weary, these things would please no longer. And when everything about us is too indifferent and monotonous to engage or retain our attention, we long for occupation and change or fall asleep for want of it. In saying that the activity concerned in pleasure is doing what we please, I mean all such activity as we engage in spontaneously, our energies being fresh, and either waiting or seeking the opportunity for action. Such is the position of healthy children let loose from school. During the quiet and constraint of the morning's lessons their muscles have been rested and refreshed and now find vent in wild shouts and play.

Of such sort is the activity of a child for the first three or four years of life. All that it does it does because it is fresh and ready for the work: one advance secured, it has an interest in the next, to which it was before indifferent. It does not attempt to bite till its teeth begin to work their way through its gums, nor to articulate till it has learnt to babble, nor to walk till it can crawl. And so, doing only what it is ready to do, and, therefore, has an interest in doing, advancing under the prompting of its own growing powers, it advances with enormous rapidity. In two or three years it has learnt without trouble or fatigue a vast number of complicated movements, is practically acquainted with space, knows the properties of numerous objects and above all has acquired an intelligent command of language. This is probably a goodlier array of acquisitions than any it will have to show after ten years of school. No doubt, in all this it is helped by heredity; very naturally, our inherited experience is realized and put to use as soon as it can be useful. But this does not affect the practical lessons to be drawn from the suggested study of infancy, nay it adds to them. The child has not yet exhausted the organized heritage of his ancestors; there is a natural order of mental development and the process is still the same, from the more general and simple separations and combinations of the elements of its experience to the more complex. And, when we see how surely and thoroughly the tiny scholar advances in knowledge while this method is of necessity followed, we must allow the desirability of abiding by it still, when Nature's training begins to slacken and to need supplementing by other means. The younger the pupil is the more imperative is it for the teacher to adopt what Bain calls the psychological sequence of subjects, to direct growth that is incipient, but to avoid all forcing and the foolish haste that tries to cram with ready-prepared material, as if the time required for mastery and assimilation were time lost.

During infancy, i.e. till the seventh year or later, the mind is mainly occupied, in the way described, in mastering the rudiments of perception and movement and so much of language as this involves. What it has thus accomplished remains its permanent possession, and can be lived over again in fainter forms without the repetition of the original experience. Still more, it can be recombined in other forms independently of external presentation or actual movement, that is to say, the young child can imagine what it does not see and has not seen; but only by the aid of pictures or narratives. Imagination is as yet to a very small extent constructive: children before seven or eight have little fancy and less thought. Picture-books, nursery-rhymes and fairy-tales, if they call for no combinations of ideas more complex than those which the child has already formed and the elements of which it has experienced, and if they promote only good nature, kindly feeling, and dislike of wrong, are admirable adjuncts of toy hammers, bricks, spades and buckets. But, in my opinion, they should be only adjuncts: a child is I think receiving higher education when engaged in play of the latter kind or in ripping up and smashing the handsomely finished toys, with which unphilosophic grandmothers love to adorn their Christmas-trees. When a little child is so quiet that his mother or nurse suspects mischief, he is probably making most strides towards being a man of independent judgment and character. When he is tired of entertaining himself, then bring out the pictures, or, still better, draw new ones before his eyes. And if you tell him a tale, tell him an old one rather than always something new. For if the tale is a good one and will help to make him a man, the impressions must be deepened if they are to be fixed. Besides, everlasting novelty will tend to produce a vapid and wandering mind. I needly hardly say that all this implies an amount of individual attention which no school-teacher could afford to give, but then is it not clear that schools for children under nine or ten are only good where home education is impossible? The Kindergarten system, in the hands of one who understands it, produces admirable results, but it is apt to be too mechanical and formal. There does not seem room for the individuality of a child, to which all the free play possible should be given in the earliest years: afterwards it can more effectively take care of itself and will be less easily repressed.

The chief danger with the Kindergarten is that its rules and method should be known and applied, or rather misapplied, by persons who have either forgotten or never understood its principles. I fear there is truth in an observation of Dr Fitch's—that there is many an untrained teacher who gets "a sixpenny book about Froebel's gifts, buys a box of cubes and some coloured strips of paper, sets the children to build bricks and weave little mats, and then says that she has adopted the Kindergarten system.... The difference between the trained and untrained teacher is, that the one thinks that the mere adoption of the gifts and mechanical exercises devised by Froebel is all that is necessary in the system; the other, by getting hold of the principles which underlie the method, is in a position to devise new and appropriate methods for herself—methods and exercises probably much better adapted to the needs of English children than Froebel's, which were meant mainly for the children of German peasants."

The fundamental idea of Froebel, that of life as a unity, manifesting itself in various ways, a whole that becomes more complex by gradual development but never ceases to be a whole, has important bearings upon education at every stage, applies not only to infancy, but to childhood and youth as well. Let me briefly illustrate. We understand what we make, chairs and dolls and steam engines, because we *have* made them, put them together piece by piece, and can at any time take them to pieces and put them together again. But things that live and grow, that have never been in pieces, and that cannot be taken to pieces without for ever being destroyed—such as a plant, an animal, a mind, a nation,—are harder far to understand. We are forced to take them to pieces in imagination; mentally to analyse them and give a separate name to different organs and functions and stages of the one individual life. Where, however, are the leaves and branches and rootlets of the oak in the acorn? Where are the gay plumage— the keen sight of the kingfisher in the egg? At what moment does the child's imagination begin; when has he first a conscience or reason? Such, I take it, were the reflections which worked in Froebel's mind. To call attention to a complete scheme of education based on these ideas of the unity of life and its gradual development and organization by pamphlets, books and newspaper articles, was his main occupation for thirty years before he even started a Kindergarten. And, in fact, but for the lamentable circumstance that his own schooling had been of the scantiest description, and that he was, therefore, debarred by his ignorance of classics from finding a place in the secondary schools of his country, we might never have heard of the Kindergarten at all.

The leading principle in Froebel's educational scheme which led him to see the man in the child at play, and led him to believe that by guiding the child's play it was possible to train his mind, is nothing more or less than a great biological truth applied. And most assuredly if it be true, and if it has been fruitful, so far as infantile education goes, it is true, it is worth applying a great deal further. The child's mind, like its body, grows gradually, and the future vigour of both depends on the right food and the right exercise being applied. What is right at one time is wrong at another; it is wrong to give meat to babes or milk to men; it is wrong to teach the babe to walk before it can crawl. For the mind, too, every branch of knowledge is good in season and wrong out of season. The question is, What is the natural order, what is the psychological sequence of subjects? And, again, what will each subject do, what is its educational value? A child's body cannot make bone out of starchy food, like rice and sago, though it may make fat: and useful information and sound moral precepts will not save it from intellectual and moral rickets, though they may convert it into a splendid prig.

Now, while I believe that modern school-teachers are really beginning seriously to ponder these vital questions and even to think that some knowledge of the laws concerning the nature and development of mind might help them, yet at the best it must be long before such a thoroughgoing reform as I imagine Froebel contemplated can be actually brought about. The practical difficulties in the way are manifold; the difficulty of even seeing the truth is great. First of all, it requires a good deal of faith to put information in the second place and education in the first, to have patience to let the child's mind grow. But, leaving this aside, it is hard, I repeat, to see that what the man wants most is not what the child wants most. The mature man, bearing the heat and burden of the day, finds himself stayed or thwarted—if a merchant, perhaps because he cannot read Spanish; or if a manufacturer, because he cannot use some dye he likes without rotting the fabric —in a word, he wants knowledge. Not so the boy: what he wants first of all is exercise. If I were to say he wants play, that would be misunderstood, and yet it would be true in a sense, and the sense in which Froebel saw it and applied it. What the boy wants is to try his powers: gymnastic for his muscles and gymnastic for his mind. If you can impart the knowledge that will be useful by and by while training his mind, so much the better every way. He will not like his work the less for seeing that it will be useful. Quite the contrary. If, when you teach arithmetic, for example, you put him to find out from the data you give him how many square miles there are in his parish or how many people to the square mile; if you put him to apply his geometry in pegging out a tennis-court or finding the height of the church-spire, so much the better: he will like his lesson all the more. Yet he will be interested in the results not because they are useful, but because he has found them out by himself. This was the plan adopted by Dean Dawes, at that wonderful school of his at King's Somborne, in Hampshire, at the very time that Froebel was busy with his Kindergarten in Germany.

LECTURE III

GROWTH OF MIND (CONTINUED): CHILDHOOD AND YOUTH

By the seventh year, or thereabouts, the period of childhood may be said to have commenced. The characteristics of infancy do not all at once disappear; there is still interest enough in sensations and movements. But the novelty has diminished; old experiences are continually recurring and many are now so familiar that their charm has gone. To tear up paper boxes, and to roll cotton bobbins over the floor have ceased to be matters of absorbing interest for half an hour, because they have ceased to have anything new to disclose. A fresh trait is now apparent. Having secured the great mass of the raw material of experience and shaped it into the simplest forms, the child now begins to build up these simpler forms into others more complex: having converted the clay into bricks, its interest is, in large measure, transferred to the random heaps of these; and it begins to erect with them the outer walls of the temple of knowledge. In other words, the vast store of concrete perceptions gathered in the busy, happy days gone by now begins to engage the attention, on which the external world, less an unknown fairyland than before, makes smaller claims. The activity which was lately employed in building up perceptions and intuitions is now busy discovering a further order among these. In respect of this further order, even perceptions and intuitions are material, just as bricks are material when our end is to build a wall, though to the brickmaker they were the forms into which he moulded what would else have remained shapeless clay. This new intellectual activity the beginnings of which characterize childhood is thinking, or, more precisely, conceiving. But just as in combining sensations into perceptions the material was given to the subject attending to them, so again here. The material for conception is furnished by what is often termed the faculty of imagination of of representation. By this we must not understand any new activity of the conscious subject or thinking mind; for, in some mode or other, representation takes place whether we will or no. Representations are given to us just as their originals were; and, so far, the only activity concerned is that of attending to or receiving them. You can no more hinder a train of ideas passing through your mind than you can hinder a succession of sights and sounds being presented to your senses, as you walk along the street. The more you are interested in the one, the less you will attend to the other, though both are there through all your waking life.

As we saw in the last lecture, the impressions which the child receives and combines to-day, though crowded out of consciousness, are not crowded out of existence. It is a general law in psychology that the more intense impressions tend to draw off attention from weaker ones. It is also a general law that even when the same impression is continually presented, its intensity tends to become less and less. *Semper idem sentire ac non sentire ad idem recidunt* are the words in which Hobbes formulated this law: *it is almost all one not to feel at all and always to feel alike.* For example, the miller sleeps so long as his wheel continues in motion, but wakes up when it stands still; the occupant of the pew falls asleep during the delivery of a monotonous sermon, but wakes so soon as it ends. When, however, the external stimulation ceases, the intensity of the impression very rapidly declines.

By the action, then, of these two laws it is that the occupants of the stage of consciousness at any one moment are presently driven off; and are kept off so long as there are new arrivals of interest to take their place. But the moment this interest slackens, or the way is clear, the old impressions begin to revive, as we see perhaps best of all in our dreams. And, as when they first appeared we called them presentations, we may call them representations on their return. But we cannot execute those movements in the case of representations which we were led to make in the case of the original presentations, for you cannot pluck a remembered rose nor shake hands once more with a departed friend, however vividly both are represented to your mind. On this account, the representations have been termed 'mental residua[1],' what the mind has secured and made its own from the changing world without. They constitute, in distinction from the external world which we control only by actual movement, an internal world, which we are said to

---

[1] [The reader would do well to refer to what is said about retentiveness and imagination in *Psychological Principles* (pp. 81 *sqq.* and 169 *sqq.*). There Professor Ward points out that just as psychologists have erred in regarding the presentations of any one moment as merely a plurality of units, so they have erred concerning the so-called 'residua' of such presentations. "As we see a certain colour or a certain figure again and again, we do not go on accumulating images or representations of it, which are somewhere crowded together like shades on the banks of the Styx." What persists, he urges, is not a particular presentation, as an isolated unit, but rather the whole field of presentation as differentiated.—*Ed.*]

control by thought. What we mean by this control we shall see more clearly by and by. Let us first become a little better acquainted with this new world, which has grown up between the infant soul and that external world to which all its first interest was given. Though called into existence, in good part, by the child's own activity, yet it did not owe its existence entirely to this: it has therefore, as I have said, laws of its own. Representations or ideas will arise in his consciousness neither arranged in a logical order nor arranged so as to afford him most entertainment, but the order in which one will succeed another will depend solely upon certain quasi-mechanical relations between (i) the intensity of each representation, and (ii) its compatibility with those which have already entered within the threshold of consciousness from the vague realm beyond. Left to themselves representations go dancing through each other like the pictures in a dissolving view. How bizarre and meaningless are the products of such interaction of representations, when uncontrolled, we see in our dreams. Yet this interaction among representations admits of control in two ways; and first by suggestion. When words are spoken the representations associated with these words, if there are any, at once arise in consciousness, and others incompatible with them are excluded. It is in this way that, as we have seen, infants may be entertained by means of their imagination, that is to say, by means of the mechanism of representations just described. In the same way substantially, presentations may awaken or suggest connected representations, when there is a sufficient store of these, and the mind is sufficiently disengaged from the present impressions themselves. Some school-teachers, in withdrawing attention from the world of Nature to the world of letters, act upon the tacit assumption that mental growth is independent of converse with the external world. This was the practical position taken up till Bacon urged men to recognize "the hidden ties that bind creation's inmost energies":

> *Her vital powers, her embryo seed survey,*
> *And fling the trade in empty words away.*

Besides the forms of control by suggestion, the train of representations can be directly controlled by attention. It is this direct control by attention which we call thought in the wider sense—i.e. active imagination and logical thinking. Intellectual advance in childhood is made by means of all three.

By the aid, then, of language, by the suggestions of the world without, and by its own reflexion and fancy, the child is enabled to work up its representations into new and coherent wholes. At the outset, it stands as helpless in the presence of this new world of representations as it was at first in the presence of the world of sense and movement; and, as its progress in reducing this to order, in advancing from isolated and unrelated sensations and motions to definite perceptions and acts, was largely accelerated by the labours of those who had lived before it, so we shall find it to be here. What heredity did in the one case, language does in the other. Save for this, as instances like that of Kaspar Hauser and other children of the woods shew, the most gifted mind would never rise much above the level of a brute. Language is the chief instrument by which the residua of perceptions and actions instead of remaining a waste of "such stuff as dreams are made of," become elaborated into conceptions and ideas. Yet language in the first instance does but fix and make permanent combinations among ideas which the mind has formed without it. Language aids thought, it does not dispense with it. With this preamble, we may leave language out of account for a time, and observe the bare process of thinking without it.

Strictly speaking, that juvenile romancing and castle-building, which even the most prosaic persons must recall with delight, is a species of thought—a fact which may, perhaps, obtain for it more indulgence than it sometimes receives. For these early feats of imagination are so much more coherent than dreams as to shew plainly that the naturally random succession of ideas has been controlled; indeed, if we observe ourselves carefully—if any will confess to a weakness for reverie—we can detect ourselves actively shaping and selecting our characters and scenery. And, no doubt, children do the same. Here, again, then, we have practical applications thick upon us. All further progress, not merely intellectual but moral, depends on the elaboration of representations; and their successful elaboration depends, *caeteris paribus*, on their mobility, in other words, on a quick and lively imagination. Without this, I do not say merely that literature, geography and history must be appallingly dull, but even what are regarded as the triumphs of pure thought, the higher principles of science and philosophy, will be unattainable. Without it, too, human sympathy could not be expressed, and all fine feeling would be impossible. It is a natural mistake to suppose that because an extravagant and ungoverned imagination is antagonistic to the reasonable in thought and action, therefore, he is best off in both who has least imagination. There is another way of saving your neck besides starving your steed, and that is to learn how to manage him. A quick and lively imagination is as indispensable as quickness or fineness of sight and hearing; and, like these, can only be improved by exercise. Nature, accordingly, does well in inciting the young to a ready command of the materials of this inner world.

It must be allowed, however, that such flights of fancy as children indulge do little more than insure this command. Thought in the narrower sense it is not. If you ask me to say in a word what thought is, you must not expect a definition on which you might stake your life. Roughly speaking, at all events, and more exactly than it seems at first sight, thought may be defined as seeking the identical or similar among ideas that are partially different; or, again, as bringing together and uniting ideas that agree together. For example, when a child, familiar with bats, birds and butterflies, reflects that they all fly by means of wings and recognizes them as in this respect alike, he has been thinking: and if he connect this thought with a movement, as by flapping his arms and jumping into the air, he will have fixed his thought by the aid of a sign: flapping his arms and jumping in the air will now be for him a symbolic representation of all the variety of bats, birds and butterflies he has seen or will see. Of course, unless he is dumb, he will hardly adopt such an unwieldy symbol; language will save him trouble by suggesting a much simpler movement, that of pronouncing the word wing-fliers. Not, however, that any such symbol is essential to a single act of thought so simple; but it can hardly be dispensed with, if the ideas brought together are to remain united. If, now, the child compare wing-fliers with arrows and with kites, and recognize that even these widely different objects agree in being things that fly, this new ground of agreement between things before disconnected, whereby further classification of his experiences is possible, will be a new thought. And, in this way, he may proceed in other directions recognizing first those things that have most in common and thus forming small classes, which he may combine again, so far as they are similar, into larger classes; and so on continually.

At the risk of being tedious, I must dwell on this matter somewhat more in detail. What I want above everything to impress is the paramount importance of the educator keeping close to the order of mental development. The mind can only grow by degrees; it cannot comprehend the agreement, or form a conception combining facts of a more general kind, till it has first combined facts more concrete and less general, whose more obvious points of identity are sooner evident. Just so often as it is forced to skip these earlier steps, just so often will confusion be the result. The psychological character of such confusion we must defer to another lecture. I only desire now, in this general survey, to lay stress on the necessity of giving time for each stage in the mental development being consolidated in its turn. To hurry over foundations because they are out of sight is to produce a structure like Nebuchadnezzar's image: a head of fine gold on feet of miry clay. The more lofty the structure we intend, the more needful is it that it should have good understandings.

Now, in thinking there are two difficulties: (i) we can only attend to a few things or ideas at once; (ii) it is harder to recognize identity the more it is overlaid with diversity. On both accounts, therefore, it is plain that real thinking can only advance gradually, and, indeed, very gradually. Having learnt to perceive the quality of roundness in its hoop, a child will identify the same form in a wheel notwithstanding its spokes, then in a plate and a penny, although so much less in size, then in a bun, though the form is here less perfect, and the matter too interesting for much attention to mere form; and thus, at length, the conception of roundness becomes clear, and by means of this the differences of round objects fall out of sight, the multiplicity becomes a unity. When similar groups of three-cornered things and square things have been formed, the young thinker may, by and by, rise to the more general conception of shape, a conception which it could by no possibility have reached directly. For now the lower concepts, round, three-cornered, square etc. stand out by themselves as single objects to which, so soon as the child's mind is familiar with them, he can attend as easily as he could to a hoop, a plate, a penny, before: and as the differences in colour, size, material and what not, do not enter into these higher complexes, round, three-cornered, square etc., the points in which they resemble each other —occupation of space and the possession of bounding lines—are recognized, and thus the general conception of figure or shape is attained.

When the materials for the formation of a concept are sufficiently prepared in the child's mind to make the recognition of their points of agreement possible, he is sure to experience pleasure when he is led to see the identity even by direct suggestion, in which case the child is said to understand. And his pleasure will be greater still when the resemblance is the result of a comparison he has himself instituted, which case more properly deserves to be called thought. Left to themselves, however, most children, at all events, will make but slow progress, partly for want of the aid of language, partly for want of the necessary juxtaposition of the material. But, though they need help, they should not be helped too much. They may seem to get on faster when everything is well done for them, but the permanent efficiency of their minds will be less. Their bodies never grow so fast as when by some accident they are confined for a time to their beds, when though they might have been less in stature they would have been more robust if they had had to support their own weight. The most careful and comprehensible teaching, widely as it differs from stocking the memory with words and phrases, does not come up to the ideal of mental training: it imparts sound instruction but it does not do all that can be done to give sinews to the mind. Rousseau's observations on this point are excellent. "Our unlucky facility in cheating ourselves with words that we do not understand begins," he says, "earlier than we suppose"; and, accordingly, he suggests that a child's vocabulary should be kept as limited as possible, lest it should have more words than concepts for the words to symbolize; its nurse is to be strictly forbidden to din useless words into its ears.

The more we depend for the attainment of our end on the child's activity, the more imperatively necessary is it, however, to secure his interest. Not much good will come of irksome thinking: the mind set down to an uncongenial task will expand about as much as a sea-anemone would in vinegar. What, then, is the nature of *intellectual interest*? The pleasures of memory, the pleasures of hope, the pleasures of imagination have long been favourite themes, but I am not at this moment aware of anyone who has attempted to sing the pleasure of thinking. Yet thinking has its pleasures, and pleasures too which children, if wisely handled, keenly enjoy.

One of its pleasures arises from what Professor Bain is fond of calling "*the flash of identification* between things never before regarded as alike"; in other words, the pleasure of novelty, a pleasure which, as I have said, is much enhanced, when the discovery has been our own. In place of the novelty at first supplied by new perceptions comes the novelty of finding new bonds of connexion among these to keep up the interest in knowledge. How real this pleasure is is evidenced by the classic instance of Archimedes which has given the word 'Eureka' a place in the English dictionary. And the admiration people are never tried of expressing as often as they contemplate Newton's inimitable discovery of universal gravitation is further proof of the pleasing wonderment all minds feel in the detection of unexpected likeness, in finding the one in the many. A more familiar illustration of the same thing we see in sallies of wit, the gist of which also lies in the surprise of an unsuspected resemblance. On this account, Jean Paul Richter warmly recommends that children should be encouraged to be witty and he even kept a book with the title "Anthology of my Scholars," in which he recorded every successful stroke of wit his pupils had made, not omitting jokes directed against himself. Some of these were very clever, although nobody that I know of has followed Jean Paul's example. Perhaps, however, the most important evidence of the pleasure of intellectual exercise for our purpose is that manifested by children who succeed in the problems one sets them: in addition to the fairly intellectual pleasure of simplification, there is the pleasure of power. On this point I will digress for a moment to make a practical remark which a little tact ought to impress on every teacher, but which none the less the habit of regarding mainly absolute results leads many to overlook. With the school-teacher (as with a general and his soldiers) the standing rule should be: Never let your pupils suffer a defeat, if only because defeat demoralizes. Of course, like most prescriptions, this fails sometimes, and is moreover to be taken with a grain of salt: sometimes, for example, overweening confidence needs to be checked, sometimes temporary defeat ensures more lasting victory in the end. But, whoever has often contrasted the brightness and liveliness of children who succeed with the downcast and puzzled looks of those who can make no way must be convinced that the one class have gained, and the other lost, interest in their subject or confidence in themselves, or both. "The inclination of the mind," says Locke in a passage in his Journal, "is as the palate to the stomach: that seldom digests well...or adds much strength to the body that nauseates the palate and is not recommended by it." The persistence of such mental disgust is amazing, as most of us perhaps can testify, and I am satisfied that many a lifelong dislike and incapacity for a subject has been due to an inauspicious beginning.

The Jesuits, as I daresay many of you know, had a practice which would astonish some modern school-teachers: they kept a register of marks indicating each scholar's proficiency—and the boys who got least marks got least work. The plan was really a most philosophical one: where all try, work should be adapted to capacity and then all alike taste the pleasure of success, and so, to adopt Locke's simile, soon increase their appetite for work. "At the entrance upon any sort of knowledge," as Locke has elsewhere said, "when everything of itself is difficult, the great use and skill of a teacher is to make all as easy as he can."

But, returning from this digression to the nature of intellectual interest, there is still an aspect more important than the pleasure of the flash of identification and the pleasure of success: I mean the pleasure of satisfied curiosity. Wonder, it is said, is the parent of knowledge. Of this emotion children for the most part shew no lack, before they go to school at all events; then, perhaps, the need of imbibing what they are not expected to understand cures them of their thirst for knowledge.

The curiosity of the child is to be distinguished from the interest the infant finds, in acquainting itself with the sensible properties of all it can see and touch. Curiosity implies a consciousness of ignorance on some definite point and a desire for enlightenment. Even a further distinction is possible, that which the Germans sometimes express by the words *Neugier* and *Wissbegier*: curiosity to know, for example, how a given story will end and curiosity to know, say, how it is that the moon does not shine every night, as the sun shines every day, or why ladies keep on their bonnets in church while gentlemen take their hats off. It is this latter curiosity that is of interest to us, because it is a powerful motive to intellectual activity. And here, for the first time, we come upon an activity determined by a definite want, an intellectual *hunger*. This curiosity is characteristic of a somewhat later period of childhood than that in which the formation of concepts begins. Not that children never ask troublesome and puzzling questions much earlier than this; but, for the most part, the relations of things are indifferent to them until they have progressed far enough in the process of conceiving to be able to think about the things themselves. Then thought awakens the desire for knowledge. And this necessitates a new return to the world without. What is wanted now are propositions not concepts; propositions stating the reasons or causes or purposes of the events and arrangements perceived, the how and why of what is or happens. Now, I do not say that education is to consist merely in judiciously aiding the child to satisfy this craving in the irregular fashion in which it will naturally arise: though this is no small matter, and many have been the men of eminence who have attributed their success to sympathetic aid to thought thus casually rendered. But this alone is rather supplying material for growth than directing the growth itself. All I wish to insist on is that you cannot advantageously begin to train a child in a branch of knowledge about the subject-matter of which he has at the time no curiosity and in which his interest cannot, or cannot yet, be awakened. If the subject is one he must learn, because of its utility, well and good: learning must here be a duty: but the full fruits of intellectual training can only be secured from work that is a pleasure. There is no branch of knowledge which cannot be made an efficient instrument of intellectual culture in the hands of a sufficiently able teacher and for those who desire to master it. One cannot have lived much among men without seeing that powers which have been developed in one case by the study of classics have been developed in others by the study of mathematics. Not, however, that this makes one-sided study desirable: far from it, as these men are the first to admit. Where nothing *better* can be done, as the less of two evils, the pupil might receive his chief intellectual training when his activity can be most counted on, even though it is one-sided. Yet there is hardly any limit to the variety of interests that may be called into activity in most children of average capacity, if their curiosity is wisely directed at the outset. This, however, requires an amount of care and attention that can only be given at home and is one more argument for home education at first.

The secret of securing interest in varied forms of knowledge is to secure a variety of concepts: there can be no desire for knowledge where there has been no thought about the things to be known. The condition of all-round culture is all-round training from the first: training for all the senses, a stock of perceptions as wide and varied as the world can give; then, the discovery of resemblances among the innumerable particulars and the first steps towards classification; and then, so soon as the concept or class-notion has been formed, the acquisition of a name by which the materials brought together may be held together and a new advance made possible. The need is for laying the foundations *all round*, and for making possible regular advance. It is customary with architects in their specifications to direct that all the walls of a building shall be raised to the same height together: the builder may not carry up a side wall as high as the eaves and let the front wall remain built no higher than the plinth or, perhaps, without even the foundations cleared. It is unnatural when you have been working with your trowel as high as the chimney tops to descend once more to the ground; moreover, if you do, the new wall cannot now without great pains and trouble be bonded into the old, and even should this be accomplished after a fashion, the result will only be that either the new wall or the old will crack. The reason why so many have now to lament the one-sidedness of their intellectual interests is either that they were allowed or caused to advance when children in one direction, instead of advancing in all *pari passu*. With many parents and teachers in the present day, one-sidedness, instead of being discouraged, is deliberately fostered. Because the man who can do one thing well is the man the world wants and pays and honours, therefore they at once direct all the child's energies into that channel in which he seems most likely to attain pre-eminence, just as gardeners do when they leave only the biggest pear on a tree, hoping with this one, when monstrous grown, to win a prize. Now, though this procedure secures certain obvious advantages to society, and so to the individual whose fitness for special functions makes him valuable, yet the disadvantages to him as a man, and not as a money-maker or a marvel, are even more obvious, and we may, therefore, be sure that the gain even to the world is not a real gain. But, again, one-sidedness in the child is often the consequence of one-sidedness in parents or teacher. This is strikingly illustrated in that interesting book to which I have already referred, Galton's *English Men of Science*. We cannot suppose that an innate taste for science is more general among Scotch children than English, but in Scotland the university programme and the general method of teaching are much more suited to men of a scientific bent of mind than those in England. Accordingly, Galton found the cases in which scientific tastes were traced to teachers to be ten times more numerous among his Scotch correspondents than among his English. If children are left to grow up without observing large classes of facts that are really under their eyes and without acquiring even the names of such as they notice for themselves, one-sidedness is as inevitable as blindness would be if their eyes were always bandaged.

But I have been a great deal more discursive than I had meant to be or ought to have been. Besides beginning to think and awakening to a desire for thought-knowledge or truths, the material of science, childhood advances upon infancy in two other respects, in forming a clear perception of time and a distinct consciousness of being a self or person, with a memory of what it has lived through in the past and an expectation of great things to be done in the future. Yet this sense of personality is primarily important in connexion with moral training and may be deferred for the present.

In youth, as distinct from childhood, i.e. in the period beginning about the fifteenth year, the intellectual advance calls for little special remark. Concepts of a more abstract kind are possible, and the danger, not insignificant even in childhood, of acquiring words loosely without doing the work of thinking, which the word should but fix, is now greater than ever. For the concepts learnt later are concepts formed by the comparison of other concepts, so that the symbols of the one may be used as equivalent in certain cases for the symbols of the others by an imitative knack, without the real significance of any being known. Terms like 'house' and 'cow' you cannot remain long in the dark about. But terms such as 'nation,' 'law,' 'force,' may be easily used without any clear knowledge of their meaning, still more terms like 'nature,' 'justice,' 'life.' The isolated truths concerning the causes and connexions of things become in youth the material for a higher order of elaboration; inference and systematic thinking begin, and the cogency of argument is distinctly felt. It is very remarkable how late this form of mental activity sometimes appears. Children can often be brought to see the meaning of each step in an argument, the conclusion as well as the rest, yet a little cross-examination will disclose the fact that they do not assent to the conclusion because they assent to the premises, but because they see its truth in a particular instance or take it on authority. On this ground, I should myself incline to defer the teaching even of Euclid until such time as there is clear evidence that the scholar can reason, that is to say, see the truth of one proposition to follow from the truth of a series of others. Meantime, much geometric knowledge of a valuable kind educationally could be acquired by direct intuition: if, indeed, Euclid should not be superseded by modern geometries altogether. Feeling for proof, a sense of logical cogency, is of all things one that the educator should spare no pains to develop; but he will do this best by waiting till the feeling arises. Rousseau was in this respect, I think, wiser than Locke, in urging, contrary to Locke's advice, that to reason with children, before they reason themselves, is to make them disputatious, not logical.

The most important characteristics of youth pertain, however, to the moral rather than the intellectual side of mind. It is not so much shaping their minds as shaping their characters that is the great business now. Childhood is reasonable, though it does not reason, and is easily led; but youth, though it reasons, nay, partly because it reasons, for reason suggests superiority to authority, is turbulent and troublesome: in manhood sweet reasonableness returns. The proverbial maxims of most people recognize this fact: school-teachers, who only know the lawless youth and not the man master of himself, are apt to forget it. But for the present we must defer the consideration of this point. I propose returning to this and cognate matters later on.

And now I have said all that the limitations of these lectures will allow me to say about the general nature and growth of mind, and I have insisted sufficiently, at every opportunity, upon the necessity of always keeping this fact of growth in view. "There is nothing in the mind that was not first in the senses," said a scholastic philosopher. "Nothing," added Leibniz, "but the mind itself." The additional clause must be allowed. But this 'mind itself' stands for nothing but the subject who attends and feels; what it attends to, both in thought and action, have come into the mind through the senses, including therein bodily movements. My thoughts are mine, my acts are mine; but only because I have combined them out of material which was not mine but only given to me. This mind by itself is, as Kant well said, the poorest of all concepts; what has worth is the mind's contents, the fruits of the talents entrusted to its use. To despise these, because in their crudest form they are mere sensations and movements, is folly, and yet a folly which psychology has not so far succeeded in scaring away. Nevertheless, these words of Professor Bain are hardly overstated: "If we did not originally feel the difference between light and dark, black and white, red and yellow, there would be no visible scenes for us to remember: with the amplest endowment of retentiveness, the outer world could not enter into our recollection; the blank of sensation is a blank of memory. Yet further. The minuteness or delicacy of the feeling of difference is the measure of the variety and multitude of our primary impressions, and, therefore, of our stored-up recollections. He that hears only twelve discriminated notes on the musical scale has his remembrance of sounds bounded by these; he that feels a hundred sensible differences has his ideas or recollections of sounds multiplied in the same proportion. The retentive power works up to the height of the discriminative power; it can do no more.... This is the deepest foundation of disparity of intellectual character, as well as of variety in likings and pursuits. If, from the beginning, one man can interpolate five shades of discrimination of colour where another can feel but one transition, the careers of the two men are foreshadowed and will be widely apart[1]."

[1] *Education as a Science* (Intern. Scientific Series), 2nd ed., 1879, p. 16.

LECTURE IV

PERCEPTION OF OBJECTS AND TRAINING
TO OBSERVE

The perception of an external object, say that of a book lying on the table before us, is very far indeed from being the simple matter it is ordinarily supposed to be. If I were to say that it is as far from being the most elementary mental presentation or impression as a molecule of albumen is from being the most elementary chemical particle I should probably not exceed the truth. It is not so near to being elementary as a hundred is to being one. To pass over the number of visible points that make up the book and the table, and the distinction of the one set from the other, (i) the recognition of the book as a solid body involves the residua of numerous sensations of touch and feelings of resisted movement, (ii) the recognition of its position as external implies knowing one's own body as an object different from other objects, (iii) the recognition of its form implies movements first of the hands, then of the eyes, and a knowledge of the relations of these movements to each other, and (iv) the recognition of its distance also requires a combined action of both eyes, and a knowledge of the space traversed, to which this convergence of the axes of both eyes corresponds. Not only are all these features involved in such a perception, but they must have been experienced many times over, and in many connexions, before that stage can be reached in which, as with ourselves, perceiving a book on a table entails no conscious effort at all. The young mind has to go through all these stages, and to go through them frequently, before it can perceive things as adults can[1].

The proposal of the Pestalozzians to place geometrical figures and copies of the Apollo Belvedere round the infant's cradle, that it might begin early to improve each shining hour and its tiny mind, manifests a surprising ignorance of the most patent psychological facts. It was, on this account, originally my intention to unfold the matter at length, and point out one by one the stages in the long journey from elementary sensations and movements to the perception of objects and their qualities or characteristics. And this, not so much from its psychological importance as because

[1] [See Note at end of this Lecture.—Ed.]

it seemed the most impressive way of exhibiting the fact that children have a great deal more to do in learning to use their senses than those who have forgotten the lesson at all suppose. But I find I must rest content with a less thoroughgoing method, and endeavour, when the time comes, to make my point clear rather by examples than by principles.

Training in the perception of objects is often called training of the senses or training to observe. This phrase 'training of the senses' is extremely ambiguous, not to say inaccurate, and to it a good deal of the confusion that exists is due. One finds the subject not seldom discussed under the head of physical education! And rightly, possibly, if what is meant is merely such a training as a tea-taster or a letter-sorter or a piano-tuner undergoes; and there have been writers who have advocated, and schoolmasters who have practised—Basedow, for example—the training of the senses thus literally understood. The ability to discriminate slight differences of intensity or quality in sensations of the same sense is by no means an ability to despise. A man dull of sense is very often a man whose senses are dull, but we cannot infer from that, that if we could render him as keen of sight and hearing as a savage, we should sharpen his wits in the same proportion, or even at all. We should certainly add to his stock of materials, but whether he would work up this material into knowledge would depend upon his interest in it. On the other hand, if, in due time, we awaken an interest in the objects perceived through the senses, so that these objects are more attentively observed, we shall no doubt bring about a considerable improvement in the bodily organs of sense.

The senses of sight and touch, together with the movements of the eyes and hands, are our chief natural instruments of observation. The ear occupies distinctly a second place intellectually; though it makes up for this in two ways, (*a*) because spoken language is impossible without it, and (*b*) because it is *par excellence* the emotional sense. The deaf have no equivalent for the charms of music, the beauty of poetic melody and rhythm, and the tender or stirring tones of the living voice: and it has been remarked that the deaf are more apt than other people to be cruel without provocation[1]—indeed, we are all familiar with Shakespeare's dictum that "a man who has not music in his soul is fit for treasons, stratagems and spoils." All these senses, often called the 'higher senses,' deserve to be cultivated; but they will be cultivated best in connexion

[1] Theodore Waitz, *Allgemeine Pädagogik*, p. 49, *n.*

with the interests to which they minister: hearing, chiefly in learning music and learning to sing and recite, and the other senses in acquiring a face-to-face or intuitional knowledge of external things, and the sensible changes they effect and undergo.

It is with this concrete knowledge of the world about us, that is, with the things in it and the events which happen, that we have now to do. Roughly speaking, we may say that the perception of a *thing* implies the perception of resistance, position, form, size, number and arrangement of parts, texture, colour, and so forth; that the perception of an *event* implies the perception of motion— i.e. change of position or change of form—either of the whole or parts, and changes of intensity in the quality and rate of these changes. Thus, we perceive the resistance even of the air, when we run, when we compress it in a bag or invert a bottle in water; of water, when we row or swim; of solids, when we endeavour to change their form; and so we perceive matter generally by its resistance to our muscular effort. Position, size, form, again, we perceive by movements combined with successions of touches or sights, as when we step the distance between the wickets at cricket, measure the width of a doorway by extending our arms, or follow with the finger or with the eye the outline of a vase. And so, generally, we perceive all that concerns objects in space by connecting sensations and movements. Motion, as change of position and change of form, which is, of course, also change of position, implies not only space but time. This, again, is due to a combination of perceptions of the present position or form with the continuously fainter residua of the series of perceived positions or forms assumed by the object in passing from its old position to its new one. Number involves a further complication of the same elements: we want a succession of movements and *halts*, as when counting on the fingers, and the discontinuous positions or halts must be taken together and yet kept distinct. The perception of a quality as definite implies a comparison of it with some other taken as the standard quality for the time, as when we compare a blue with the blue of the sky, or determine it by reference to a series of blues, as when we call it light, medium, or dark.

It ought, then, to be abundantly plain that the acquisition of such knowledge, though it incidentally implies a physical training of the senses, is itself an active intellectual exercise. Training in this sense is, moreover, the only intellectual training possible to a child before it has acquired some considerable command of language and independent control of its ideas. Further, it is the best and surest way of attaining to this higher development. And nothing can be more absurd than to suppose it is not necessary. In one way, certainly it is not necessary. If sound in sense and limb, even a child left to run the streets acquires a knowledge both of things and their names. But its knowledge in the one case is at least as defective as it is in the other; and the systematic training, which is allowed to be needful and useful for the second, is just as needful and useful for the first.

The point I desire, however, chiefly to insist upon is not so much the knowledge gained as the mental quickening. By a judicious training in observation, you begin to make a child think when it is five years old[1]. But, if the child is left to itself till it is seven or eight, and then put to learn spelling and tables, it is really so smothered under a mass of crude and shapeless ideas, loosely strung to a tangle of vague words, that thinking is impossible. There are a few animals in the world that can eat hard for a whole summer, and then, after a good sleep, grow into something lively and handsome; but these are grubs and not children. If a child is to think to any purpose, he must think as he goes on; as soon as the material he has gathered begins to oppress him, he must begin to think it into shape, or it will tend to smother intellectual life at its dawn, as a bee is drowned in its own honey for want of cells in which to store it. Yet, on the other hand, nowhere is it more true than here: to him that hath shall be given and he shall have more abundantly. Nothing makes us so capable of more knowledge as knowledge already assimilated. Nevertheless, to let the years slip by, when everything is fresh and activity is abounding, without directing and fostering the budding desire to appropriate and comprehend, is the easiest and safest way to make a dullard of even a bright child.

Neglect of facts so obvious may be explained in three ways, (*a*) through the general ignorance and distaste for natural science which has prevailed until lately, (*b*) through the equally general ignorance and contempt for the study of mind which prevails still, (*c*) through the enormous inertia that pertains to all educational institutions. There are scores of men, who ought to know better, who evidently imagine that comparing the structure of different

---

[1] This is the gist of the contentions of Pestalozzi and Froebel, and they deserve all the honour they seem at last in a fair way to receive. The pity is that they have spoiled a good idea by a mechanical treatment of details.

flowers, or studying the physical geography of the surrounding country, is little better than a means of keeping the more stupid boys out of mischief: "the boys," as one schoolmaster says, "who can never hope to sail in the great language-ship and see the world." In music, French, drawing, and natural science, says this writer, the most backward in classics can take refuge! How thankful we should be for small mercies. Such a man, it is quite clear, never dreams that long before his great language-ship is fit for sea, long before the beautiful feats of mental gymnastics—the Latin hexameters and the Greek iambics, which he admires so unreservedly—are possible at all, exercises of intellect, the same in kind with those which afterwards engage us when handling abstracter and subtler subjects, may be begun. Because a man is said to use his senses when he observes, observation is confounded with sensation, which is about as wise as confounding art with paint-brushes. The reason why intellectual training—for that is what this so-called sense-training really is—can begin sooner with sensible objects is not merely that these are the first material which the mind secures, but that the conceptions it forms are so much more distinct when the objects that embody them are before the senses. All life through, we feel that we can realize best what we are thinking about when we realize it literally by being face to face with the facts. But this is much more important for children, whose constructive imagination is feeble and uncertain.

Besides the advantage of holding from the first a shaping and formative attitude towards the material furnished by the senses, there is a further one still, and one no less important. Observation cannot be done by proxy, and a child judiciously trained to see or verify for himself is much more likely to rely upon himself, and know the full meaning of truth, than one trained only through books, who receives more on trust, and is, therefore, more in danger of blind deference to authority, and what follows upon this—excessive dogmatism. In this way, the study of facts corrects one disadvantage of the study of literature.

Let us, however, now turn to the psychological conditions of a training in sense-knowledge. The general rule is here, as in all cases, to follow the order of mental development. And this I have represented to you as a synthetic order, a building up of a more complex mental object out of others more simple, as when the colour and scent of a violet are associated with its shape in our perception of the flower. But this generally synthetic procedure is crossed by another and apparently opposite one. Though what is always presented together among changing circumstances is grouped together as one thing, yet the constituents of the group are not known as definitely at first as they can be afterwards, when the senses have been more exercised and attention can be more concentrated. The child works over its material, therefore, a second time, and finds differences that had escaped it at first: it mentally takes to pieces its perceptions and attends to the elements by themselves. It calls, at first, everybody 'father' who presents the same general outline; later on, it distinguishes some characteristic mark it had overlooked before; and, connecting this henceforward with the vaguer outline, by such means knows its father from other men. This procedure is called analytical by the logicians, because they regard it as resolving a whole into its parts; but psychologically, as it occurs in the growth of the child's mind, it too is synthetical: it is merely adding on a further and a distinguishing element. Notwithstanding, we shall do well to call it analytical: that is, the process of learning more precisely the parts or properties of an object; and then reserve the term synthesis for the process of connecting together into classes the things that resemble each other. Training in observation will furnish opportunities for an exercise in both, though more especially in the former.

Besides seeking to elicit at first only the more important properties in an object and its more obvious relations to others, successful training, especially in the case of young children, will require a good deal of time and patience both for the first appropriation of the new knowledge and for securely fixing it in the mind. If I were a school-inspector, I think I should require those who teach the alphabet to take a lesson a day in reading unpointed Hebrew, or in describing accurately the form of all the Hebrew letters; it would bring home to them what a business it is to master a lot of new symbols. What is true of this most nauseating business is true also of one equally interesting, that of object-lessons. Even when they single out things for themselves, children want time to have a good look at them before they take them in. And what they have distinctly noticed one day requires to be renewed—though, perhaps, to keep up interest, in some slightly different circumstances—the next, or the first impressions will soon fade away. Too much repetition at one time is useless and worse than useless, because tiresome for everybody. The secret of Japanese lacquer is, I believe, to put on many coats, but only one, very thin, at one time: and this would be the best policy even if all you wanted to do was to lacquer your pupils. Impressions are best fixed by the interest that attracts attention to them; and, when this has been once attained, it is the wiser plan to let the tide of interest lead attention to the next point, taking care that the advance is gradual and consecutive. Then, among associations connected with the lesson will be these: (*a*) how interesting! (*b*) how short! A lesson with such pleasant associations it will afterwards be a pleasure to revise, especially if the accessory circumstances are re-arranged; and so, with attention again fresh, the impression may be deepened, and a further pleasant association formed, the pleasure of successful reproduction.

The facts observed should, of course, at once be fixed in language; until this is done the observation can hardly be called complete. To train the powers of observation is, indeed, one of the surest and best ways of acquiring the accurate use of language. Still, they should not, as Pestalozzi supposed, be regarded as a means to this end; on the contrary, language must wait on knowledge of fact, not knowledge of fact on language. Intimately as the two are connected, there can be no doubt as to which is prior,—no doubt, at least, except after a very long time spent in producing those, as Mr Thring, the schoolmaster I was referring to a little while ago, calls them, "splendid specimens of training and of power to make the mind perform its master's bidding," modern Latin verse and Greek iambics, which, though, as he is good enough to tell us, "they cannot be named in rivalry with Wordsworth, Tennyson, and the poets of the day," he seems to think are especially fitted to drill into graceful shape "the luxuriant power of higher thought and an intense vision of truth." The way to higher thought doubtless requires the mastery of language. Yet, this is to be obtained not by a cunning skill in the manipulation of synonyms and epithets, despite the trammels of metre, and their being in a dead language, and to express the ideas of others, but by acquiring words and using them when face to face with Nature, in the moment of discovering the truth the words are to enshrine. The vision of truth, whether intense enough for pitiful poetasters or not, determines the want for which words are to be ready as soon as they are wanted. Precise and accurate such words must be, and, here, pupils depend almost entirely upon the teacher, for, to whatever purpose they use their eyes, they cannot, by the light of Nature, discern the names for what they see. Much, indeed, of the lack of power to observe is due to the too general inability of parents and tutors to supply inquiring little philosophers with the words they need to fix the facts they have observed. "What is the name of this little thing?" a mother is asked. "Ah, it is some nasty insect, child, throw it away, or perhaps you'd better kill it," is the reply. And the next capture, whose different shape and manners attract the child's watchful eyes, is denounced in severer tones as a nasty insect too; until, after a little of such admirable training, the child acquires a wholesome and comfortable indifference to nasty insects or unpleasantly smelling weeds, and submits instead to learn his spelling and to earn a cake.

With young children, whose fitful interests and disconnected experience necessitate desultory teaching, any person, not disgracefully ignorant, may be always ready to help them to use their senses. But, when regular work is possible, and especially with higher classes, random lessons on objects must give place to something more systematic. This entails careful preparation on the teacher's part to avoid a number of practical difficulties, such as "unseasonable and uncontrolled digression," which is the besetting sin of the object-lesson, as Professor Bain truly remarks. The psychological aspect of some of these difficulties will come up for notice as we proceed. At present, I will content myself with the remark that the more a teacher is concerned to educate rather than merely to inform the safer he will be from the many failures that beset the attempt to give what are called object-lessons, or generally, to give instruction in science.

Let me conclude this lecture with a saying from Rousseau's *Émile*, which I might have taken as its motto: "Since all that enters into the human mind comes into it by way of the senses, man's first reason is a sensitive reason; it is this which takes the place of the intellectual reason; our first masters in philosophy are our feet, our hands, and our eyes."

NOTE ON THE NATURE OF PERCEPTION

[This Lecture was unfortunately left in a more incomplete condition than any of the others; and it is certain that the brief paragraph with which it opens would have been considerably expanded in delivery. What is here said about the process of perceiving objects needs to be supplemented by reference to Chapter VI of *Psychological Principles*. There, by the ingenious device of taking as the subject of treatment a typified individual who is regarded as having continuously advanced from the beginning of psychical life to those forms of it with which we are most familiar, Professor Ward was enabled to leave aside, through-out the greater part of the volume, the awkward questions relating to heredity, and thus to avoid the sort of objections that the remarks at the end of the first paragraph of the present Lecture are calculated to awaken.

In unfolding the nature of perception in the chapter of *Psychological Principles* referred to, Professor Ward follows three main lines of con-sideration bearing on (*a*) the recognition or assimilation of impressions, (*b*) the localization of them, and (*c*) the intuition of things.

As regards the first, the great difference is emphasized between what these terms, recognition and assimilation, denote in the case of the simplest mental processes and in the case of the more complex and developed. Just as the 'pure sensation' is a psychological myth, so the simple image, or such sensation revived, is equally mythical. As a matter of fact, the subsequent sensation is not like that which preceded it; it is a change in the field of consciousness that has itself been changed by what has gone before; and it cannot properly be said to reproduce the past sensations, because they never had the individuality which such reproduction implies. In short, what is ordinarily called recognition is preceded by recognition or assimilation of a much more rudimentary kind, and it is this latter that would be operative·in the mind of a young child.

With reference to the localization of impressions, Professor Ward lays stress upon what he designated the 'extensity' of sensations—what Bain had named 'massiveness'—an original characteristic, in his view, which forms the basis upon which the experience of extension or space is developed. And it may be noted that this characteristic of 'extensity' would of itself serve to differentiate 'sensations' from mental states or modifications. The manner is then indicated in which, through the aid of 'local signs,' and more particularly in virtue of bodily movement, positions in space come gradually to be distinguished. The function discharged by active and passive touch in the tactual apprehension of space is dwelt upon, and it is shewn how active touches come at length to be 'projected,' while passive touches are alone localized in the stricter sense. Finally, the important part played by the joint operation of the two eyes in the visual apprehension of form, shape and distance is dis-cussed, and the mode of the gradual development of the 'stereoscopic vision' of man is traced.

But perhaps the most distinctive part of Professor Ward's account of perception is contained in what he writes about the 'intuition of things.' There are, he points out, in the complex percept of a physical thing a number of features that call for psychological consideration. (*a*) The perceived object is said to be actual or real; and by actuality or reality, in this context, is meant that which is opposed to the ideal or the merely represented. The difference, it is argued, turns solely upon that which distinguishes the presentation from the representation of a thing's qualities or relations, and this depends partly upon the relation of the presentation of the thing to other presentations that are apprehended along with it, and partly upon the attitude which it evokes in the apprehending subject. As William James put it, real fire will burn real sticks and give out heat, whereas we do not attempt to light real sticks by ideal or imagined fire or to warm ourselves thereby. (*b*) In the apprehension of external things as solid and impenetrable, it is the experience of resistance to bodily movement that is the primordial factor. At the outset, things are for the conscious subject all corporeal like his own body, which is for him the first and archetypal thing; their solidity is clearly experienced only when active touch is accompanied with effort. Moreover, in addition to muscular effort, simultaneous sensations of contact are essential for yielding the distinct presentation of something resistant, occupying the space which the body has been prevented from occupying. (*c*) The object is apprehended as *one* thing with many qualities, and such apprehension comes about through the same group being presented again and again in the midst of changed surroundings. "There is nothing in its first experience to tell the infant that the song of the bird does *not* inhere in the hawthorn whence the notes proceed, and that the fragrance of the mayflower does. It is only where a group, as a whole, has been found to change its position relatively to other groups, and to be—in general—independent of changes of position among them, that such complexes can become distinct unities, a world of many things." (*d*) In reference to the apprehension of a thing as permanent, stress is laid upon the significance of the body as alike the earliest form of self and the first datum for our later conceptions of permanence and individuality. We transfer a permanence like that of the bodily self to other bodies, and, without the continuous presentation of such a group as the bodily self, we should never have been prompted to convert the discontinuous presentations of external things into a continuity of existence. (*e*) Finally, the substantiality of a thing in the midst of varying attributes comes to be recognized as the tangible plenum, as that which occupies space, the constituent in the complex which is invariable, while its form alters, its colour disappears with light, its sound and smell are intermittent.

Thus, then, the idea we form of a real external object extends in all its features beyond the content of any given sense-presentation; it is clear that what we call perception is a highly complex and variable process, and that the final result, that which is relatively the most familiar to us, involves the co-operation of a very considerable number of the simpler processes of mind. If we seek to indicate by general names what are the processes most fundamental in perception as a whole, we might, perhaps, say that they are (*a*) discrimination, whereby the particular presented content is singled out from its concomitants, (*b*) assimilation, whereby that content receives the additional definiteness due to bringing to bear upon it any previous like experiences, and (*c*) localization, whereby there is assigned to the presented content a certain position in space. But these terms, when taken in the abstract, convey a very imperfect idea of what is peculiar to the process of perceiving. What is really of significance lies not so much in the distinguishable mental functions as in the nature of the combined factors, whether immediate presentations or representations or concepts, which come together and yield by degrees a more or less adequate interpretation of each sense-presentation.—*Ed.*]

LECTURE V

RETENTIVENESS, REPRODUCTION AND IMAGINATION

So far we have been mainly concerned with presentation and the reproduction and control of what remains of old presentations under the influence of new ones. But the development of our minds would soon stop if we could not get this power into our own hands, if we could not recollect what we have known in the past, but had to wait till some new event suggested it, or if we could not think connectedly except so far as actually present objects gave us clues. This is very much the position of a child for a time. Let us, then, see how this mental mechanism of ideation, as it is sometimes called, acts; and what we can do with it.

And first of Memory, which, of course, is purely a matter of ideation and not of sensation. If, when asked the date of the founding of Rome, the very question at once brings the answer 753 B.C., you are said to remember; if you have to think first and only at length recover it by some absurd mnemonic connecting the city of seven hills with 700 B.C., plus the next lower odd number—750, plus the next lower odd number again—753, you are said to recollect. But the process, so far as ideation is concerned, is the same in each case: in the first the representation was direct and independent of any effort on your part, in the second it was indirect and dependent on an intervening series of other representations. This difference we may leave out of sight for the present. In memory there are, then, two things: (*a*) retentiveness, or the possibility of representation, (*b*) reproduction or actual representation. Both are essential to remembering but the conditions of the two are different. Many retain long who do not quickly recall; others can almost instantly recall what they retain, yet retain but little for long. One man goes into an examination and fails to recollect, although, six months afterwards, when himself more collected, he can recall with ease, the knowledge that a second had then at his fingers' ends and has since worn off. Most people must frequently have found themselves unable to recollect some name which they still feel they know, and often one has heard the somewhat Irish remark: "I remember it perfectly but I forget it just now." Few, indeed, are the orators who deliver a speech without finding that their best points have a provoking way of recurring to them the moment they sit down. The distinction between retention and recurrence is, then, I trust, clear.

Retentiveness is evidently the more fundamental fact; for we may retain what we never reproduce, though we cannot possibly reproduce what we do not retain. That an impression once attended to is ever lost is more than we can prove; and, certainly, there are many startling instances recorded of languages learnt in infancy, and apparently utterly forgotten and quite beyond recall by any voluntary effort, recurring spontaneously when the ideation mechanism is urged to more excited action by delirium or fever[1]. Even though an impression made long ago may never return *so far as to be recognized*, for such recognition is implied in memory, it may still form part of our mental furniture, just as a man who is lost in a crowd still helps to make up the crowd though we do not succeed in distinguishing him again. And, no doubt, a very great deal of our experience is of this form, and the practical consequences, so far as character is concerned, are of the greatest moment. The grass does more than the trees to make the earth look green, and the little things we do and suppose done with tell more, perhaps, upon our lives than the important steps we regard as everything. It is because of these little things, at once lost in the crowd, that a man of forty is, as the proverb says, a bundle of habits. However, what we are now interested in is rather those more impressive presentations that are distinct enough to be recognized, if they do recur. How is it that some of these are retained and remembered and others disappear from distinct consciousness for ever? Other things being equal, an impression is more likely to be retained (*a*) the more intensely, and (*b*) the more frequently it is presented. The conditions of retention are thus mainly physiological. Supposing we considered it handsome, as some noble savages do, to cut pretty figures on our cheeks and arms, we should find it best to cut them early, deeply and repeatedly, if we would be beautiful for ever. Now, what we see taking place in such a sacrificing of the skin is very much what takes place in the brain; and, just as we might call a scar the memory of a wound, we may suppose that, so long as an impression is retained by the mind, the brain has become permanently modified, so that though its substance changes the old marks remain. But the modification

[1] *Cf.* Carpenter's *Mental Physiology*, chapter x.

is, of course, a natural change of growth leading to an increased activity or readiness to act.

I always feel a certain repugnance to speaking thus of the brain in connexion with the mind, because such exposition is so apt to be construed in a materialistic sense. And yet the strict parallelism between the states of the two is too evident to be overlooked. Thought is not matter in motion and cannot be conceived as such. However deeply I dive into my own mind, I shall never come upon a motion of molecules instead of a succession of ideas and impressions; however far the physiologist dissects and analyses, he will never get beyond the fineness of nerve-structure and nerve-currents so as to reach the quality and intensity of the sensation. Keeping this great gulf in sight, then, it may be useful to learn indirectly from physiology that which the study of mind does not directly teach us; or, at any rate, does not enforce so strongly—what we may call, therefore, the physical conditions of acquisition.

In the few words I said about physical education, in the second Lecture, I ventured to point out the need the growing brain has for frequent rest. I may here, while speaking again upon the same subject, point out from this side the inadvisability of brain-forcing. Even when rest is secured, *time* is required for growth; and it is a far sounder and healthier plan where facts have to be acquired to let them, as people say, work into the mind gradually, i.e. grow, than to require an exact repetition, say, of lists of irregular verbs as fast as they can be learnt by heart. Another point—this work of committing to memory is not physically the easy matter it is supposed to be; the memory is not a waxen tablet upon which we can almost instantaneously impress whatever marks we may wish to remain. Memoriter lessons especially call not only for attention but for a fresh and vigorous brain. Yet, very generally, I believe, lessons to be learnt by heart are prepared at night. This I cannot help thinking is a mistake. The best time for such work is surely in the morning, when the brain is fresh and the attention is no longer distracted by the events of the day or oppressed by a sense of weariness. No doubt, it would be a gain to read the lessons over aloud carefully and deliberately at the close of the day. This ensures them comparatively undisturbed lodgment, so that the work of ingraining can begin; but the morning, I feel sure, is the time for deepening and fixing the impression. But, however learnt, revision should not be too long deferred, especially with young children; for, in a rapidly growing brain, old traces soon disappear like footsteps upon moving sand. No matter how indelibly some event in our past experience is fixed, though we are sure that as long as we live we shall never forget it, yet we do in strictness forget it the greater part of our time. What, under such circumstances, i.e. when there is no doubt about the retention, are the conditions of reproduction?

Sometimes, representations of the past seem to revive not only unbidden but apparently without reason. Lounging upon some bank where the wild thyme grows, numberless happy scenes surround us again, scenes of the long-forgotten past, which have revived without any effort on our part, or any suggestion that we can detect in what is present. But, in fact, we should find, if we cared to examine, two reasons at least for this reproduction, (*a*) that our mind was free from the class of thoughts with which our daily life is occupied—work and care neither oppress nor depress us; and (*b*) that the change of ideas though rapid and often sudden is yet never between any two moments complete. In other words (*a*) the way is clear for a new set of ideas, and (*b*) such new ideas arise as are in harmony with our mood and position and as are linked together by some association.

It is this association together of particular ideas that we have chiefly to study; but I should like, first, to say a word about the power which moods and feelings and the larger interests of life have to shut off, as it were, a whole region of ideas and bar it out entirely from access to the light of consciousness. Strong emotions exclude from the mind all ideas incompatible with them; fear calls up its troop of spectres and sanguine hope shuts out the view of difficulties and dangers. In the same way, strong interests, and because they imply corresponding emotions, give a ready entrance to all that relates to the one fixed idea, as it is called. The miser is all attention when gold is in question; the collector is roused from indifference at the mention of Roman pottery or rare autographs. Such strong emotions or interests become a sort of other self, and one to which the real self is often freely sacrificed. The worth of a man, in fact, consists in the interests for which he is enthusiastic; we do not think highly of the man whose self-love is so cool that no interests whatever can induce him to sacrifice his personal happiness. But it is not my intention to pursue this fact of our nature into all its practical applications now. I only want to remark its bearing on the acquisition of knowledge. Observe the conduct of a powerful man, say a king, with his ministers and with his friends. His intimacy with the former lasts so long as they further the ends for which they are the means, when their work is done they are dismissed; and, perhaps, they are at once valued and disliked, as is a good doctor by a gouty patient. Yet his intimacy with his friends and favourites is the staple of his life; they are ever with him and all that he has is theirs. So is it with knowledge acquired for its own sake, as contrasted with knowledge acquired as a means to secure reward and avert punishment. The knowledge we delight in we keep ever about us as our body-guard, and know it intimately and on all sides; whatever furthers it is learned with avidity; our attention and time are gladly spent upon it and the work is a pleasure. What we learn because we must may, however, very possibly—not necessarily, by any means—be afterwards associated with pain and boredom, and, therefore, gladly banished from sight; the ill-usage boys sometimes bestow on their school-books is but the expression of such a feeling. So we see in yet another light the importance of awakening and main-taining in the young an interest in knowledge generally, and, at least, in some branch of knowledge. For, as I have said before, an interest in any of the great branches of knowledge will make a good intellectual training possible, where the teacher is efficient.

The reproduction of representations, then, depends in general on the emotions or interests with which we are possessed at the time; ideas not consonant with these are apt to be struck out alto-gether; but more particularly—the reproduction of any particular idea depends immediately upon its association with other particular ideas. It is this second and more purely intellectual condition of reproduction that we have chiefly to deal with now. The laws of such association are expounded and illustrated at length by Pro-fessor Bain; but fundamentally they are all, I think, reducible to that which he treats first—namely, the law of contiguity, that the mental residua of objects which have been presented together tend to reproduce each other in the original order. In this way, to imagine the smell of tar, and still more, of course, the actual smell itself, will lead many of us to think of fishermen and their nets and boats and the sea stretching away beyond, not because there is necessarily any connexion between tar and fishing, or tar and the sea, but simply because we have in the past experienced the two together. There are no ideas which cannot in this way become associated so that one calls up that which accompanied or followed it, except such as cannot be in consciousness either together or in immediate succession. It is to this primary law of association that we must, in the main, refer what we call the memory of our past life. If the several connexions were lost, though the elements were retained, we should not be said to remember. As when, for example, the pictures of half a dozen cathedrals rise in my mind but I can no longer say where I saw the originals. Nay, even though I could also recall the cities to which they really belong—so that there is nothing lacking in the arrangement, all the materials to arrange being there—still this would be a case of forgetting. Strictly speaking, of course, some material has been lost. What we call the link of association between two objects must always be itself an object; but it may be, and probably is, an object supremely unimportant. Between important objects such comparatively unimportant objects are always intervening, between things and words to which we attend come others to which we are comparatively inattentive. Hence, after a time, in consequence of the law of obliviscence, which I mentioned before—the law, I mean, that mental residua, while in the region of subconsciousness steadily fade in intensity and as it were melt away—in consequence of this law, I say, the fainter links fall out and the originally continuous series becomes resolved into fragments.

Now, this disintegrating action of obliviscence, though sometimes an inconvenience, is, on the whole, a gain; and to attempt to make such forgetfulness impossible is a great mistake. For the breaking up of the original, more or less accidental, associations makes the process of associating things according to their deeper and more important relations all the easier. What sort of place would a museum be in which all the specimens were arranged in order of their arrival instead of being distributed according to some system? The power to recall a long string of events or words in the order in which they were originally presented is often called mechanical memory. Mr Latham calls it portative or carrying memory. It is memory in this sense that is popularly supposed to be incompatible with a high order of intellect. And, certainly, the most remarkable modern instances of wonderful memory have been furnished by idiots. Not that this proves much, nor is it on any such ground that the popular belief rests. Sir William Hamilton tries to refute the common opinion by citing instances to the contrary—as those of Grotius, Pascal, Leibniz and Euler, who were men of extraordinary memories. No one will deny that the power to retain and at will to recall what has been understood and thought out or what has enchained and interested in the past is wholly an advantage; without some considerable power of memory in this sense, it is plain, intellectual advance would be impossible. Neither can anyone deny that a man who has this power of retentiveness and ready recall will, if he choose, be able to learn *Paradise Lost* or the *Corpus Juris* by heart and repeat the whole word for word. But the point is that the constant habit of so doing, to use up one's mental energy in this fashion, is injurious. And yet this habit is one that school-teachers have encouraged and enforced with dire penalties any time these two thousand years. Psychologists might well be excused a smile at the follies due to ignorance of psychology committed by the very men who despise it, were it not that their own faulty terminology has done much to hide the truth. I should like to illustrate this point by referring to what may be called scholastic as distinct from psychological theories concerning memory. The school-teachers reasoned consistently enough after this fashion: "Memory is essential to knowledge. Memory is a distinct faculty of mind, therefore, in order to attain knowledge, the memory must be trained." Human nature protested, boys hated school, clever boys not the least, the world declared that the school-teacher's prodigies were nothing but huge sponges from which you could only squeeze out in a somewhat muddy state what they had at first imbibed. Theorists like Montaigne, Locke, Rousseau, pointed to the "sad and sterile childhood" which the prevailing *régime* produced. Yet the school-teachers had the courage of their convictions; no one shewed the flaw in their reasoning, and they continued to train the memory as of old. The truth is that memory is not one distinct faculty and understanding another. In learning a page of grammar off by heart, a boy has certain words presented to his mind in a certain order and he has to attend both to the words and to the order or relation among them; and, as they are attended to, so they are associated and retained. In *understanding* a page of grammar he has certain ideas present to his mind which he brings into special relations, and, in these relations, attends to them; and, as they are attended to, so they are associated and retained. The question, then, is not of a faculty of memory which is present in the one case and absent in the other, but of two modes in which the order of association is determined, whether it shall be that of the original presentations or an order determined by the mind for itself. Train to attentive and accurate understanding and leave the memory to take care of itself is what I should say; the more your pupils can retain and reproduce in that case the better. For you cannot exercise their understanding without improving all that is good in memory; but, in making it your first concern to strengthen their memories, as the phrase goes, the chances assuredly are that you may dwarf their intellects.

The subject is, however, educationally of such moment that I must entreat your patience if I endeavour at once to clear away any appearance of paradox that may indispose you to believe what psychology has to teach about it. First, there are some things that *have* to be learnt by heart, things one must not only understand but know the instant they are wanted. Of such, the multiplication table and sundry formulæ in common use by everybody are examples. But even here the shortest and the surest way to fix such relations in the mind is to understand them, before attempting to commit them to memory. You, no doubt, will all agree that the multiplication table ought not to be learnt till, by means of concrete objects, the child has been taught what an arithmetical operation means, and, by adding first two or more different numbers, and then two or more repetitions of the same numbers, has come to see the connexion between multiplication and addition; and, by adding first four threes and then three fours, and so on, has so far learnt the equivalence of any order of multiplying the same factors. In some cases, perhaps—though these, I believe, are fewer, the abler the teacher—rules have to be learnt by heart and verified by applying them, before the pupil can obtain the experience needful to the clear comprehension of the proofs. Again, some things, which we are obliged to know, have no reason, but then it should be remembered that such have so far no educational value. As long as we have our present miscalled orthography and barbarous medley of weights and measures, children must toil through dreary spelling-books, and work hosts of examples in reduction, practice, compound addition, etc. Yet, even here, a wise teacher will succeed in introducing a good deal of method; and the more method there is the less there is for memory to do, the more there is remembered by being understood, the less there is remembered mechanically. Further, the things about which the child has to learn facts by heart will, at all events, be seen and handled. The children will not have to learn, as I expect most of us did, that sixteen ounces make a pound, and take their chance of ever coming across the common ounce and pound of commerce, which have so long been their enemies. In all these cases, however, seeing and understanding is not enough, learning by heart is necessary; here it is, I admit, not enough to train the understanding and leave the memory to take care of itself. Still, even here, it would be absurd not to reduce the mere memory work to a minimum, under the notion of strengthening an important faculty.

There is yet a second and quite distinct case in which learning by heart to a moderate extent is commendable; I refer to committing to memory passages of good prose and poetry, but here again such only as can be understood. Human beings are largely imitative, and especially are they imitative where taste and dexterity are involved; so that familiarity with good models is good not only in itself but as a protection against the unconscious influence of bad models. Still, in my opinion, no piece should be committed to memory till it has first received an exposition adapted to the pupil's understanding and stage of culture. Further, the practice of learning much by heart even then, unless counterbalanced by composition and criticism, so soon as these are possible, will produce an unnatural style, full of mannerisms and conceits.

Accordingly, in all cases, learning by heart is only justifiable as a means to an end; it is not an end in itself, it does not afford any general educational training. The power to remember other things will not be increased by learning off by heart the Eton Grammar or Virgil's *Georgics*; nay, it may be very well diminished. That the contrary often seems to be the case I am aware, but the explanation is easy. Actors and barristers are cited as instances of what can be accomplished by training the memory. When a barrister begins practice, he has more difficulty in carrying one brief in his head than he finds later in carrying ten. But this does not prove that he is more able at the end than at first to retain and reproduce a given series of new impressions. He does not carry his ten briefs with ease because anything that can strictly be called his memory is improved; perhaps, at the very time, he may be conscious that this is already failing him; but because the whole ten together contain less that is new and disconnected than one did when he began, and because he understands his cases considerably better than he could have done at first.

There is but one thing to justify the popular conception of a general faculty of memory, and that is what Professor Bain in his larger work calls "the natural force of adhesiveness specific to each constitution, and distinguishing one individual from another"—

of which, as I have already said, the most remarkable instances have been furnished by idiots. It is no doubt to this physical basis of memory that Locke refers when he says: "Strength of memory is owing to a happy constitution and not to any habitual improvement got by exercise." If such adhesiveness is improvable at all, it is so mainly by promoting the health and nutrition of the brain. When, from this general condition of memory, the power of the brain to be permanently modified by impressions, we pass to special conditions—such as repetition and association—we pass to conditions which are only good for the particular impressions or ideas to which they are applied. Repeating a speech from *Julius Cæsar* till I know it will not improve my general retentiveness, nor—the control of attention, which it perhaps increases, apart—will it make fewer repetitions suffice when I want to get off, say, the lunar theory. If there were one single faculty for remembering everything this would be different; if you strengthen your arms for cricket you strengthen them for rowing too, because you use the same arms in both. The power of concentrating attention, on which the vividness of an impression or idea very largely depends, *is* the same in all cases, so that, if the power is increased by learning a speech by heart, there will so far be a gain whatever has to be learnt next. But he would be a bold man who maintained that the best way to acquire control of attention is to commit strings of words to memory; I should say it is almost the worst.

Returning, then, once more, to the facts of association we have to ascertain what conditions these point to as the conditions of permanent acquisition. To utilize at once of the law of contiguity and defeat the working of obliviscence by repetition, so as to deepen the several impressions and strengthen the associations between them, is the plan we have already discussed a good deal; the German name for this, 'outward learning' (*Auswendiglernen*), is as happy as ours, 'learning by heart,' is unhappy, being intended, as ours evidently also is, to imply thoroughness. A second plan, which may be called in distinction from the first or mechanical, the artificial, is that of devising mnemonic aids or tags; innumerable schemes of which exist, most of them in modern times, I believe, the product of the revival of learning. Such schemes were sure to occur to men who could hope by an effort to carry the whole of human knowledge in their brains, and at a time when such knowledge was mostly book-lore. But, in opposition to learning by rote and learning by tricks, there remains the plan of learning by understanding, what Kant calls judicious memorizing, or, as we may say, intellectual memorizing. Now, you may be disposed to ask: why not continue all three? It is in answer to this question that I shall try to make good my assertion that, if you train the understanding, you may leave the memory to take care of itself.

First, the two plans are to a large extent incompatible. The associations formed as the result of intellectual reflection on a subject are generally reached by breaking up the associations formed by mere contiguity, and substituting others based on agreement, causation, design, and the like. It is in this way that Nature herself may be said to train all men. The objects about us have many properties alike, the events that we observe have antecedents in common, in the midst of diversity there is uniformity. Such uniformities become the occasion of a higher order of contiguity. Certain elements in one object or event recall similar elements in others and these objects being thus brought together in consciousness become associated. This is Professor Bain's law of similarity. Thus, the similarity between the petals of a flower and the leaves of a plant suggested to Oken the morphological identity of the two, that the petals, that is to say, are but modified leaves, notwithstanding the difference of colour and position. But, now, a little reflexion will shew that the stronger the original associations of contiguity the harder it will be to bring about a new association which depends on the suspension of the original one. It is thus that truths are hidden from vulgar eyes chained to the concrete and particular, while a deeper insight can penetrate beyond superficial diversity to the agreement that lies beneath. This, then, is the incompatibility which makes learning by heart a bar to learning by understanding. The habit of the one strengthens the original contiguity in which knowledge is first presented, that of the other the new arrangements which every mind makes for itself of all that it understands.

We have, perhaps, many of us seen the difference, to our own humiliation, when another by quietly thinking over things has discovered new relations among facts with which it had been our boast to be familiar for years. And how often do you find boys at school admirable so long as reproduction is enough, but hindered by the literal accuracy of their knowledge from seeing its application to a new case, which accordingly they proceed to get up *de novo* in the same wooden fashion as before. But, again, another reason for not learning by heart what is understood is that it is largely superfluous; to learn by heart what is not understood is, as I have tried to shew, injurious. The associations formed by understanding are stronger and more economical than those formed by mechanical repetition; when the one is secured, there can, therefore, as a general rule, be no need for the other. These associations are stronger, (*a*) because they are the result of a greater activity of attention; we put, as it were, more of ourselves into what we think out; and (*b*) because the associations formed are more numerous and intimate, on which account the knowledge in question is said to be assimilated and not crammed. No two minds in this respect are alike, as every teacher knows who has seen how differently different pupils handle the same problems. Different in temperament, tastes, previous knowledge and experience, to no two does the lesson present the same points of contact by which it can be most completely apprehended and retained. Each appropriates it, therefore, in his own way; and, generally, by stating it in other, and probably inferior, language, providing new illustrations and instances and rearranging the proofs; to each it presents different difficulties and suggests different applications and reflexions. Just as when a cheese falls to be divided among men, mice, and mites, they lay hold of it differently, it agrees or disagrees with them differently, they make different chemical rearrangements of its substance, till finally—if they have not taken too much at a time—the cheese and they are one; it is assimilated and not crammed.

But the associations formed by understanding are more economical, and, in this respect, again, superior to those of mere contiguity; the two are related to each other much as the master key is to the bunch of separate keys which it supersedes. The boy who simply trusts his memory, having at great pains learnt Tweedle-dum, is next, as I said just now, at as great pains to learn Tweedle-dee; but he who has grasped the mystery of Tweedle-dum finds himself thereby all but master of Tweedle-dee. If our minds and our opportunities were not finite, this would not matter so much; as it is, anything which saves us from a burden of details adds as much to our mental wealth as it would to our material wealth to be able to change a purse full of coppers for a purse full of gold. The extraordinary command of details displayed by a great statesman or a great naturalist is due not to any such habit of mind as that which memoriter lessons encourage, not to brute memory, but to a habit of systematic organization which leaves no fact isolated, to a habit of understanding as much as possible in order to leave as little as possible to remember.

The sum and substance of it all, then, is, briefly, this—the separation of memory and understanding is a psychological abstraction. In reality, the mental process is the same in all acquisition, that is to say, we attend to ideas in a certain order and, in that order, they become associated and reproduce each other. What is called training the memory is neither more nor less than strengthening the habit of attending to things in the order in which they are given; perpetuating the contiguity of presentations. Exercising the understanding, on the other hand, equally involves attention and association, and, therefore memory; but the characteristic of the mental process, in this case, is that the order of presentations is superseded, and the new ideas are incorporated among the old according to some system, which, though generically the same for all minds and so called logical, is individually different in each. How far this new knowledge can be retained and recalled depends, in the first place, on the attention given and on the strength of the associating bonds, as to both of which the superiority lies with understanding. It depends, in the second place, upon repetition; the oftener the new knowledge has been recalled the more surely and easily it can be recalled again. And here, too, the advantage is on the side of understanding. He who only acquires knowledge by understanding it recalls the old as often as it aids him in assimilating the new, and so his knowledges, to use again a useful word we have lost, become one living whole, each part of which keeps the other fresh and adds to its fruitfulness. But he who acquires knowledge by stocking his memory, places the new beside the old, like parsley and parsnips in a kitchen garden or in a dictionary. With him the letter killeth because it is afraid to die; his corns of wheat abide alone and fruit accordingly there is none.

This is the place to say something upon the subject of imagination. Psychologically, imagination is distinguished from memory only by the fact that the ideas reproduced are reproduced in new combinations and not as originally experienced. And, as there is a higher and lower, or voluntary and non-voluntary, form of memory, so there is a voluntary and non-voluntary form of imagination. In recollection we make an effort to recall the past which in memory recurs spontaneously. Similarly, in dreams, ideas present themselves to us in new guises; in imagination proper—i.e. active or constructive imagination—the new arrangement is due to effort on our part, that is, to the power we have of concentrating attention on some of the objects within the field of consciousness, and so increasing their intensity, thereby aiding their entrance into the circle of ideas associated with them; and, *pari passu*, by diminishing the intensity of the rest, of banishing them and their ideational belongings.

Of the importance of imagination, as supplementary to intellect, I have already spoken incidentally, and this will become more apparent presently. Generally stated, the vital consideration is this. All the material of our knowledge is furnished by the senses; what we retain of this material we can rearrange, independently of the external world, by imagination. In this way, therefore, if imagination is sufficiently vivid and flexible, we can, as it were, rehearse, with little time and trouble or risk, what it would be impossible or difficult to attempt in fact; so that, the more we can mature our ideas in this manner, the fewer will be our aimless and fruitless actions and experiments. We shall be like an engineer who makes sketches on paper before he proceeds to a model of his design. Or, in other cases, as in history or travel, imagination is our artist to depict, on the mental stage or canvas, scenes for which the most masterly verbal descriptions are but stage directions or rough outlines. The importance of cultivating imagination is, therefore, clear, and will become increasingly so from the discussions in which we are about to engage.

LECTURE VI

THINKING, ABSTRACTION AND
GENERALIZATION

We come now to deal with thought proper, that is, to the formation of general concepts and the processes of judging and reasoning. I have already referred to these a good deal, and naturally. For is not the whole end of intellectual training to ensure the power to think and the habit of thinking? But we must now approach this whole subject more directly.

Thought is the subject-matter of two different sciences, with both of which the educator should be acquainted, if he is to see clearly what he has to do and how he is to do it. These sciences are, of course, psychology and logic. Roughly speaking, we may say the former expounds to us how men actually think, the latter how they ought to think: the one gives us the fact, the other the ideal. A similar parallel may be drawn, and, indeed, has been drawn, between psychology and ethics, and again between psychology and æsthetics, so far as such a science can be said to exist. Psychology explains, as a positive science, how men do think, act, and admire; logic, ethics and æsthetics, as normative sciences, sciences of the ideal, how men ought to think and act, and what they ought to admire. The teacher who has to shape the growing mind should, then, as I have said, be distinctly acquainted with both the tendencies he has to correct and the ideals towards which he has to direct. We have thus to consider natural thinking, regulated or logical thinking, and the differences and difficulties that separate the one from the other.

The first steps in thought, those by which we reach concepts of the lowest degree of generality, do not carry us far enough away from the concrete to bring out the disparity between natural and logical thinking. We can all see the resemblance between a goose and a swallow; and, leaving out of account or abstracting from the differences in size, form, habits, etc., can make the name 'bird,' given at first to one, serve as the general name for both. This process of abstraction and generalization logic represents as the same, no matter how far we have advanced from concrete realities and when imagination can no longer construct definite images corresponding to our words. We start with two or more smaller classes, having respectively the marks $ABCD$, $ABEF$, $ABLM$; and, abstracting from the differences CD, EF, LM, generalize the resemblances AB into a new concept. But the actual thinking which may be thus symbolized will be very different according as AB stands for something which we can readily picture, such as a sea-animal, or something which imagination cannot depict, such as civilization, development. And there is little doubt that logic has exerted a perturbing influence on the progress of psychology by leading psychologists to substitute the more precise and definite account of thinking given by the ideal science for descriptions of thinking as it actually takes place.

Logic supposes every concept to be the result of an explicit comparison, so that the objects which it denotes, of which it may be affirmed, can be divided off from others; and so that the properties or attributes or marks which it connotes or signifies can be distinctly stated, or, in other words, its meaning be defined. And, so far as we do perform such operations for ourselves, we can fairly conform to these requirements. The great mass of mankind, however, get their concepts ready made. They know *some* of the facts or objects which these concepts denote, and *some* of the marks or attributes of the objects which they connote, or may, for aught they know, connote. Nobody has brought home to the world this fact with such force as Socrates, about whose admirable method everybody will know something, so soon as everybody is not obliged to learn Greek. Instead of our concepts, then, being formed by that sort of thinking which they represent for the logician, instead of being reached by abstraction and generalization, we obtain them by a process of unscientific induction, or even by mere custom without thought at all. We may discover this process at work in very young children by the mistakes they fall into. But it is certain to slip more and more out of sight as they come to use language of a more general and abstract kind, unless those who have to educate them see carefully to the contrary. Again, thought, as logic conceives it, takes no account of the continuous flux of representations, and of our limited powers of attention. Yet both these tell in our actual thinking. At one moment, the aspects of some fact uppermost in our mind may be, say, $abcdef$; and, with these in mind, we affirm so and so. By and by, abc may have fallen into the background and have been replaced by ghk, so that now the fact engaging our thought is present in imagination as $defghk$; and we affirm something of it which we should have seen to be false had not *a b c* slipped out of sight.

Thus, while logic takes account of no difficulties arising from imagination or language, but substitutes symbols in place of the complex image formed by the association of a word and an idea or vague group of ideas, in actual thinking it is with this complex that we have really to deal.

In proceeding, now, to discuss the relation of thought to imagination, and the relation of thought to language, I will raise first the somewhat puzzling question, what, then, is thought itself, thought apart from imagination and language? The answer is, it is not really anything at all; it is an abstraction. There may be thought in which sensible ideas may be present without symbols, and thought in which symbols are present without sensible ideas, as in algebra. All that one wishes to imply in distinguishing thought from the symbols and images employed in thinking is that thought is an activity, and that these are the material and instruments employed therein. Thought is an activity, then, of the self or subject to whom impressions and ideas are presented; and, like all activities, it is called into exercise by motives, by pleasure or pain; we think because urged to do so by curiosity, or because oppressed by an apparent contradiction, or because we desire to devise the means to the attainment to some end. It is substantially true to say that in thinking the material with which we deal is, in the first place, as I have said already, the mechanism of ideation, the train of ideas that rise above the threshold of consciousness in irregular but unbroken succession during all our conscious life. I call this a mechanism, of course, only in a figurative sense, because, though it is not determined by the interaction of *physical* forces, yet the mode in which one idea recalls another associated with it and repels any others that are incompatible is, in effect, comparable with the action of a force. The more intense an idea the greater its effects in helping or hindering the rise of other ideas; the more intimate the association between two ideas, the more rapidly does the rise of the one follow the other, and so on. This mechanism it is, I say, with which we are really concerned in thinking; for, when we turn from our ideas to the actual world of objects and events, it is to verify what we have already thought, or to obtain new ideas with which to continue our thinking. One more preliminary remark and I have done. Thought in the stricter sense must be distinguished from fancy or fiction, which is quite as difficult and quite as interesting and involves thought by the way. The difference lies in the immediate motive; in elaborating poetry and fiction, the aim is to please, to produce the beautiful; in thought, the aim is to reach truth.

Let us, then, now consider, for a moment, what language is and how it aids thinking. Words or articulations are physiologically nothing but the result of muscular movements and involve the expenditure of muscular energy, just as truly as writing or playing the piano. They are, too, the result of voluntary movements; we do not speak, as our heart beats, whether we will or no. Before uttering a word we have an image of the word, that is to say, feel ourselves uttering it faintly, and the actual utterance is but an intensifying of this image or nascent movement. And, just as by attending to an idea it becomes more distinct, so by attending to the idea of uttering a word we get near to uttering or actually do utter it. It would be difficult without occupying a good deal of time to make this clearer. Some evidence of the close connexion between the idea and the act you can see in the habit of illiterate persons to think and read aloud; and again in the fascination of a precipice. But the point I wish to emphasize is that the image of a word is not merely that of a sound, the residuum of an impression received from the external world, but also and chiefly the image of a movement, the residuum of an impression made *on* the external world. It is what I should call a motor and not a sensory representation. Yet, of all our mental imagery those of our bodily movements are most under control; we can instantly imagine any movement it is in our power to perform, and of all bodily movements those of the vocal organs are among the easiest to make.

In this lies, I think, one of the helps of language; in giving a thing a name we give it a handle—not a physical one, of course, but one by which we can mentally 'apprehend' it, whenever we will. For, by pronouncing the name when the object is present, the two—name and thing—necessarily become associated, so that by means of the name we can recall the object to mind, when without it this would be difficult. Of this you can readily convince yourselves. But not only do names furnish us with a readier command of our ideas in this sense, they also enable us to give form and fixity to the results of our thinking. A word is always a definite articulation, to which, therefore, there corresponds a definite mental image. This mental image of the word, accordingly, like

a magnet among iron filings, constitutes a strong bond of association among the elements we combine together in a thought. Save
for the *word* 'house' it would be impossible to keep together and
keep distinct from other experiences all that 'house' implies.

A name is not, however, a mere handle or bond distinct from the
thing named; it is to all intents and purposes an attribute of the
thing or fact itself. The sight of an orange does not more immediately, nor as immediately, suggest its taste or feel, as it suggests
its name. Nay, we might even go further and say that, just as
among the qualities or marks of a thing, as it exists in the external
world, there is one which we exalt above the rest and call not an
attribute but body or substance, so it is with the name among our
ideas. As we often say, we embody our thought in words. And
as it is not the matter or substance of an object that chiefly interests
us, but the qualities, so it is not the name but the meaning which
the name embodies that concerns us when we think.

However, before we inquire further what we understand by the
meaning of a word, we shall do well to look at the imaginative side
of thought. When we have seen a number of objects, such as a
herd of cows in a field, we can, it is said, compare these with each
other, recognize their points of resemblance, and abstract from or
overlook their individual differences. Now, what is present to the
mind as the result of such a process? This was long a burning
question among philosophers and logicians, and I fear to some
extent is so still. Having seen some hundreds of cows of various
colours and in various positions, when you now think of a cow
does your imagination present you with a picture of some particular cow, or with an image, for the most part vague and blurred,
in which nothing is distinct but such features as are common
to all cows? For my part, I believe the latter to be the truer
answer, and that, without any conscious comparison and abstraction on our side, in the simpler and more frequent cases, Nature
herself provides us with such generic images, as they have been
called, by the mere working of our ideational mechanism. For,
by reason of their identical elements, images of similar objects
reproduce each other, and the result of a number of such repro-
ductions will be a new image in which the uniform feature will be
heightened, while those features that vary widely from one particular
image to another will neutralize each other and produce a blur.
As is well known, Galton likened such 'generic images' to the
composite portraits obtained by superimposing a number of photo-

graphic impressions, taken from different members of a class (e.g. criminals), whereby common features become accentuated, and so a typical form produced. The objections urged against this view by the nominalists, as they are called—those who deny the possibility of a general image—prove too much. The arguments advanced to prove that a generic image is impossible would prove that any image at all is impossible. The element of time needs, in this connexion, to be emphasized. The longer we allow an idea to remain the more definite it becomes, within limits of course.

In its most elementary stages, then, at all events, instead of the generalization and abstraction of the logician, we have the combination of the features common to many images and mutual blurring or neutralization of such exceptional features as conflict with these. For example, all the swans we know being white, our generic image of a swan represents it definitely as white; but hens, being of all colours, our generic image of a hen presents no definite colour.

Now, psychologically regarded, all words that have a meaning, that is, all except proper names, and even these are not strictly exceptions, correspond to such generic images or images formed from them. Of the higher stages of thought, however, the word 'image' is apt to convey a false impression. All I mean is that when the word is understood there is, as it were, a certain movement of ideas in correspondence with the word. And when writers like Locke exhort us, in our private study, to lay words aside and "have an immediate converse with the ideas of things," they propose to us to concentrate our attention upon the generic images and the movement of these that the words bring about, rather than upon the words themselves. We must, however, avoid a common mistake here, which the expression I have just used suggests. Words do not merely correspond to complexes of ideas in imagination, but control these, and determine their movements.

Words, then, though they are indispensable aids to thought may yet prove impediments. How is this? An illustration may make both assertions clear. In a library or museum, besides the books or objects in the cases, the assistants have boxes of slips on which are written the descriptions or titles. It is plain, in this case, that in taking stock, or rearranging, there would be a great saving of labour in working through the boxes of slips, rather than overhauling the cases themselves. But, in that way, any imperfection in the titles or the loss of any volume would be overlooked. The

Birds of Aristophanes or his *Frogs*, for example, might get among the zoological books, or some old bones might have crumbled away on the shelves and be represented only by their label. Much the same holds with regard to words: in fact we might say that, as imagination enables us to save time in our dealings with the external world, so words enable us to save time in dealing with imagination. Leibniz has expressed the same thing as follows: "Just as in large commerical towns, or in games of hazard, and the like, money is not passed continually to and fro but instead of it bills or counters are used, till the final reckoning comes, so the understanding deals with the images of things, especially when there is much thinking to be done; that is to say, it uses signs instead of them, that it may not be necessary afresh to call up the thing to mind every time it occurs." And you may remember Hobbes' famous dictum, "words are wise men's counters...but they are the money of fools."

We cannot, however, begin with this symbolic thinking. We must first manipulate the ideas, just as we cannot begin with ideas but must first have impressions. Nevertheless, having obtained images from these, we can combine them in new ways, and then go to the external world to see if there is aught to correspond; so, having symbols for our thoughts, we can combine our symbols and then call up the images corresponding to the combination to see if our symbolic combination is conceivable. The reason why we can do this is clear. Assuming that we have brought our ideas into order, so that they are related each to each systematically, as are the books in a classified library or the specimens in a scientific collection, then the names of our ideas will, by the same process, be brought into a corresponding order, like the slips in the box catalogues; the names, in fact, having been a chief means of bringing the arrangement about. That this will be so follows from the general laws of association to which words are no exception. If, by thinking, we bring two objects together because of some relation of likeness, causation, or what not, so that they are associated, then their names, which are attributes of the objects, as we have seen, will be associated too. So far as this is accomplished, we may then concentrate attention on the names and let all the other attributes fall into the background. By this means, since we can only attend to a few things at a time, we have a more complete command over the objects of our thought so *far as their names and the relations established among these represent them*: so far, I say, but so far only. If, instead of saying, that in war the weaker have always recourse to negotiation, we should happen to say, that they have always recourse to conquest, the custom which we have acquired of attributing certain relations to ideas still follows the words, and makes us immediately perceive the absurdity of that proposition.

Now, there are certain cases in which the relation of the symbols to each other corresponds completely and in all respects to the real relations symbolized; and, in these cases, we can not only dispense altogether with imagery but advance beyond the resources of our imagination. Such is the case with arithmetic and algebra. We can form an image of five, perhaps of ten, but soon reach the obscure image of many. Here, in mathematics I mean, thought is purely symbolical, we think by means of a system of signs entirely: but, here, again, the same fact meets us as before. We can only attend to a few signs at a time; every simplification of our symbols makes, therefore, a further advance of thought possible; as we see, for example, in the substitution of Arabic for Roman numerals in arithmetic, algebraic symbols and operations for definite constructions in geometry, and so on.

Logic—at least that portion of it called pure, formal, or symbolic, logic—is an exact science like mathematics, though a much more fundamental one. Only some of our ideas are related quantitatively, but all involve logical relations. The work of thought in its completeness is, as we have seen, to form the material of our experience into an organized whole: the process consists in connecting like with like, overlooking special differences in each case, and picking out and comprehending general agreements, and repeating the process again and again. The result of such a process would be a thoroughgoing classification, perhaps worthless in all other respects save the one of being systematic; what Jeremy Bentham called the "matchless beauty of the Ramean tree." We may say, generally, that it is with such a formal arrangement and what it implies that logic has to do, and *that* formal exactness which logic secures by employing symbols in place of ideas we must strive to secure, when arranging not empty symbols, in which we have nothing to attend to except the form, but concepts, it may be, of extreme complexity. It is in this way that we divide and conquer, master first the formal problem of thinking and then seek to realize it in the matter of thought. So far as we succeed, our thought will be consistent with itself and will hold together as a whole.

Now, a word or term in such a logical system denotes certain objects or facts or relations; that is to say, it notes or marks them off from other things, so that its range in the system extends over them and no further: such things, or rather the subordinate classes including them, constitute its extension. But the term denotes these things or classes for a definite reason; they may have many properties in common, but it is for some assigned properties at once common and peculiar that the name is given. These properties are called the connotation of the term, and sometimes its intension, or, still plainer, its meaning.

We may now turn to the bearing of such a logical scheme upon actual concrete thinking. First, we observe that steadily as the intension decreases the extension increases. At the one extreme we have individual objects which have only a proper name, and the nearer we are to this lower extreme the more danger there is in thinking symbolically, but also the easier is it to check symbolic thinking by actually depicting in imagination what is thought about; and as we get into the region of more general conceptions, where this check is more difficult to apply, the danger is less. Moreover, in this region, if our logical structure is complete, our system of symbols itself furnishes a check. Again, what is really the same thing from another point of view, in explaining the more concrete terms we do best first to point out their denotation; but, with the more general, we must try to give their connotation. Thus, if in answer to the question "What is a bird?" I say sparrows are birds, a child will be less liable afterwards to make mistakes as to the meaning of 'bird' than it would to mistake the meaning of 'animal,' if when it asked "What is an animal?" I replied sparrows are animals. It is just from such correct but misleading applications of words that children, unless carefully taught, acquire their notions of what the more general words in common language mean or connote. Even the trivial example I have just used will illustrate this. A great many children confine the word 'animal' to mammals; or, at any rate, object to men at one end of the scale and beetles at the other being denoted by this term. But we have no choice at the outset, that is with young children, to whom all thought is new, and with beginners in a new subject: we must first point out the things denoted before we can make clear what, in these things, it is that is connoted. In this respect the often quoted dictum of Newton is appropriate: *in addiscendis scientiis exempla plus prosunt quam praecepta*: learners are more helped by examples than by rules. And after all the stress I have laid on bringing the young scholar face to face with the facts of the world and exercising his imagination with concrete recombinations of these spoils, I trust I shall not be misunderstood if I now urge that the educator must not stop at this. Vitally important as it is that the pupil should have wealth of imagery—for, as Kant said, concepts without images are empty words—yet he cannot cope with this imagery in the concrete, he cannot see the wood for the trees: as Kant adds, images without concepts are blind. Examples, then, will not take the place of definitions; and, if supplied in the first instance, it must only be as the material from which the definition is to be obtained. The man who only knows that such and such an object is denoted by a term without knowing its meaning uses great swelling words of vanity, while his inmost thought is contemptible. He talks of the relations of Church and State, when all he is thinking of is increasing the church-rate to raise the parish beadle a suit of gold lace.

But, besides the impossibility of method and system among ideas, so long as only the denotation of terms is known, there is the further difficulty, already referred to, that as soon as children—and not only children, but others too—have some acquaintance with the denotation of a term they proceed to make inferences as to the connotation. And, perhaps, of all the sources of confusion in the world this is the greatest: this fact it was which led to Richelieu's cynical remark that language was devised to conceal thought. The general explanation of the fact is clearly afforded by the inadequacy of symbols together with the circumstance that, over and above the qualities connoted by a term (the essential attributes as logicians say), there are others following from these but not peculiar to the class (called properties), and others again belonging to some objects in the class but not to all (called accidents). Now, out of all of these a selection may be made, as chance or the prejudice or interest of each determines. Supposing the essential attributes of all objects included in a class X to be AB, the properties following from these to be $a\alpha\dots b\beta\dots$ and the accidents to be xyz, one person may take the meaning of X to be $A\beta$, another Ax, another Bz, and so on. Or, take the King of Bantam, an inhabitant of the North Pole, the Prince of Salamanders, an ardent teetotaller and his favourite aversion, the publican, and compare their views on water.

Yet, indispensable as it is that the scholar should know the meanings of the words he uses and not merely to what objects they will apply, it is nevertheless extremely difficult to give the exacter logical training. "It would," as Professor Bain well says, "serve nearly all the purposes of the teacher to know the best means of overcoming the repugnance and the abstruseness of general knowledge." One requisite assuredly is that the teacher should be himself master of his subject, not only in itself but as an instrument of education. He must know what it can do and how to arrange it so as to make it efficient: what is the logical order of its parts, what are the salient features to bring to the fore and what the perplexing details and accidents to suppress. As to the repugnance to general knowledge, it is, I think, in good measure due to the dazed feeling of having to play blind-man's buff with everything, which is produced by being suddenly plunged into a cloud of general terms without the possibility of orientation, if I might use the word, or of finding one's bearings. The remedy here, I suppose, is expressed in the hackneyed phrase "advancing from the known to the unknown." A mind well stored with particulars, whether of concrete objects or generalizations of a lower order, does not object to the disclosure of a class attribute among these. On the contrary, there is the pleasure of identification, the relief of thereby overcoming an intellectual burden and the sense of increased power that ensues.

To the abstruse or obscure character of general knowledge much the same remarks apply. No doubt, sooner or later, a point is reached where, either from want of interest or from want of ability, the process of abstraction begins to halt. Either the present charm of concrete facts is too great or the effective desire of increased knowledge is too small to support a prolonged abstinence from the living realities, even to insure a diviner insight in the end. Or, even concrete facts are seen through a glass darkly, so that by and by no generic images are produced, but only an indistinguishable blur. Still, I fear that often, long before the limits of possible achievement are reached in an individual case, general knowledge is voted dry and meaningless because time has not been taken for the formation of the requisite ideas nor any regular method of advance adopted

LECTURE VII

INTELLECTUAL AND LOGICAL TRAINING

A very brief summary of the chief points of the last lecture and their practical lessons for the educator may perhaps be not altogether superfluous. Thought is an activity dealing primarily with ideas, and aims at bringing these into an order and connexion corresponding with the order and connexion of things, as experienced not by this man or that but by men generally. Language is a sort of philosopher's stone which precipitates the fleeting and soluble imagery of thought and fixes it in solid form comparatively safe from further transmutation in the flux of consciousness. It is this, where we think for ourselves; but, when we receive the words of others without corresponding thought of our own, such forms are hollow and yet opaque: they make a dreadful rattle and keep out a deal of light[1]. Hence the desirability of rather stinting the supply of this useful but dangerous article. To have fewer words than ideas is a less evil than the converse, and the habit of using words without knowing what they mean is one which the teacher should do his utmost to check. And especially is he bound to avoid himself employing terms which the pupils cannot for the present understand, or be made to understand.

But words do more than fix our concepts; they make them manageable, for our control of words is more complete than our control of ideas, so that symbolic thinking, like the fairy power of riding on gossamer, enables us to reach points of view and gain a knowledge of things which would be else impossible. Here, again, however, it is rather the danger than the gain that the teacher must attend to. His own familiarity with his subject enables him to feel quite at home gliding, as we say, with the speed of thought above the *terra firma* of concrete facts: he forgets that he ever lived upon the ground. And his poor pupils, if their interest is not stifled by disgust, come groping after him like bean

---

[1] Cp. *Faust*, Act I. Scene iv. (Taylor's translation):

> Just where fails the comprehension,
> A word steps promptly in as deputy.
> With words 'tis excellent disputing;
> Systems to words 'tis easy suiting;
> On words 'tis excellent believing;
> No word can ever lose a jot from thieving.

stalks in a cellar straining towards the light. Knowledge so attained must at best be thin and meagre, like all forced growth. Mischief of this sort is often the work of clever and conceited men and women, who are small enough to rejoice in their own mental superiority and to forget the steps by which they climbed. Since, then, we must have many impressions before we can have vivid ideas, and many ideas before we can have complete and powerful concepts, it is evident that the more haste the worse speed. Resort to the time-saving process of manipulating general terms and rules, without constant recourse to the realities symbolized, means mental collapse at a later stage. *Festina lente* should be our rule; we should advance slowly for the pupil's profit but seem ever advancing in order to retain his interest. I lay the more stress on this because of my own juvenile experience. As one of those impatient young-sters who dig up their seeds to see if they are growing, I remember having had a distinct dislike to history and translation books with long chapters and to mathematical books with long solid sets of examples. I am not sure even if it would not be worth while to make school books, as often as possible, consist of small separate volumes. To have the same dirty Arithmetic for a couple of years is apt to produce the dispiriting impression of being no forwarder. But, whatever be the risk of thinking by means of words, it is a risk we have to run. Abstraction at the same time that it is a mark of man's finiteness is also the source of his strength, and without words to fix our abstractions we should, as we have seen, rise but little above the perceptions of sense. The cardinal point, however, is to know what it is we have abstracted and to know this clearly and distinctly, that is to say, so that we shall not only not confuse it with anything else but be able to state what it contains.

This is after all the gist of the rules laid down by Descartes in his epoch-making *Treatise on Method*. Definitions as well as instances must be forthcoming if obscurity and confusion are to be avoided. To give instances of law, for example, instead of stating whether uniformity or coercion is implied, will never clear up the obscurity that invests the term. Similarly, to say England and France, Greece and Rome are civilized countries will not do much to determine whether by civilization we refer to social organization or to the progress of the arts of life, to individual culture, or what. But to insist continually on a knowledge of the meaning of words, i.e. on clear and distinct conceptions, neces-sitates gradual and regular advance. And, as I have already mentioned Descartes' method, I will quote his rules, which are to this effect:

1. Never to accept anything as true, which we do not clearly know to be so; that is to say, carefully to avoid haste or prejudice, and to comprise nothing more in our judgments than what presents itself so clearly and distinctly to the mind that we cannot have any room to doubt it.

2. To divide each difficulty we examine into as many parts as possible, or as may be required for resolving it.

3. To conduct our thoughts in an orderly manner, commencing with the most simple and easily known objects, in order to ascend by degrees to the knowledge of the most complex.

4. To make in every case enumerations so complete, and reviews so wide, that we may be sure of omitting nothing.

It may seem strange that so much stress is laid on systematic thinking. And yet the reason is evident enough. Unless we think systematically, we cannot think clearly and distinctly; and, unless we think clearly and distinctly, we do not really think at all.

It must be remembered, too, that I am not discussing the imparting of knowledge, but the training of the mind. The question what particular study will afford the best training in connected thinking and the best corrective for loose thinking is not a question for us just now. But, by whatever means obtained, such training must be afforded if education is not to fail of one of its chief ends. And, certainly, we are now in possession of sufficient bodies of reasoned knowledge to furnish such training, if only the most be made of it and of those to whom it is taught. And yet is it not pitiable to see the exhibitions even clever men are continually making of themselves—men who have been everywhere and read everything, but whose ideas, like the odds and ends of half a dozen picture puzzles in a child's toy-box, jostle each other in their brains and come to the top in their turn but never, never fit? I do not forget how much prejudice and self-interest have to do with the inconsistency of our opinions, but even prejudice and self-interest cannot pervert the multiplication table. Strong light is dry light. At all events, I cannot help suspecting that our schools and universities must largely share the blame with those ancient perverters of the truth. And, if they are to blame, it is because they make learning the first thing and thinking the second, place the tradition of knowledge before the training of the mind[1].

[1] Cp. Newman's *Lectures on Education*, p. 215.

But logical training involves something more than precision in the formation and classification of our ideas. To use the analogy most in vogue nowadays we have not only a statics but a dynamics of thought, not only a logical structure but logical function. Having elaborated our system of ideas up to a certain stage, we must use it. The products of past thought which we have embodied in words must aid in turn in the elaboration of new thought. If we thus look at thinking in progress, rather than at thought settled and complete, we shall find that we have more to do with judgments and reasonings than with concepts. The mental attitude to be acquired here is what I have already spoken of as the feeling for proof, i.e. both the need of it and the ability to appreciate it. The educator must do all in his power to develop this feeling, and to say this is to say that he must largely guide thinking, instead of supplying ready-made thought. How, then, is he to go to work? Now, there are two chief methods of exposition, (a) the method of discovery, or the heuristic method, and (b) the dogmatic method, or method of instruction. Of the latter probably the most perfect example on the whole would be found in a good text book on mathematical physics. Euclid's *Elements*, though the most convincing book in the world, is not the most systematic; it continually sacrifices the classification of its subject-matter to the exigencies of the original proof. Of the heuristic method it is not easy to mention any well-known example. And naturally it is not, because first routes are rarely the shortest, and so are abandoned and forgotten when they have made a better way possible. It will save some time, if, in order to make quite clear in what this method consists, I quote what Professor Jevons says in elucidation of it: "The method of discovery begins with facts apparent to the senses, and has the difficult task of detecting those universal laws or general principles which can only be comprehended by intellect. It has been aptly said that the method of discovery thus proceeds *from things better known to us*, or our senses (*nobis notiora*), to those which are more simple or *better known in nature* (*notiora naturae*). The method of instruction proceeds in the opposite direction, beginning with the things *notiora naturae*, and proceeding to show or explain the things *nobis notiora*. The difference is almost like that between *hiding* and *seeking*. He who has hidden a thing knows where to find it; but this is not the position of a discoverer, who has no clue except such as he may meet in his own diligent and sagacious search[1]."

[1] W. S. Jevons: *Elementary Lessons in Logic*, p. 204.

Now, it has been much disputed which of these two methods the educator should use. Pestalozzi, with his usual unbalanced enthusiasm, proclaimed the method of discovery as the only true and natural method. (Here let me observe, by the way, that whenever we find habits or institutions or methods of procedure recommended on the ground of their naturalness we need to be specially on our guard against confusion. Nature may mean almost anything. Pain is natural, Sin is natural, Custom is natural, Reason is natural. Where reason and nature are opposed, it is reason we have to follow; where they agree, reason is our justification.) Describing his method Pestalozzi says: "The child that is educated after my method, will be set down upon the road, which the first discoverer took and must have taken, and in its hand will be placed the clue which the human race itself has followed in extending and unfolding his science[1]." There is truth in this; and it deserves attention especially in view of the exclusive employment of the opposite method, universal, perhaps, in Pestalozzi's time, and still far too common. But, if it be wrong to treat the pupil's mind as a mere repository of useful knowledge arranged in the clearest and concisest form, it does not, therefore, follow that it is right to deprive him of all the advantages of past systematization. The true educational method, if there be a single method, is probably neither the one nor the other. Nature, to whom Rousseau and Pestalozzi were so fond of appealing, would have taught them better, had they lived in these days. There is much truth, I suppose most of us believe, in the hypothesis of Darwin that the present perfection of the more complex organisms, such as that of the barn-door fowl, is due to a long series of tries of which we have a partial record in certain of the lower organisms, is due, in other words, to the method of discovery. Nevertheless, if you open eggs in process of hatching, you will find Nature taking very much shorter cuts to a chicken than she took at first. Yet still there are indications of the old road, indications which make the study of embryology one of such enchanting interest. Nature roughs out the whole first, and then gradually elaborates every part, following the leading lines but not all the windings of the long and tedious process by which the primeval chicken was evolved. And this in general must be our plan; for there is, we may be sure, a profound analogy between the order in which the human race has evolved its knowledge and the order in which any given descendant of the race can

[1] See Waitz, *op. cit.* p. 331 *n.*

best appropriate it. Among the many qualifications of a first-rate teacher I should include this, a knowledge not only of his subject as it stands to-day but also of the steps by which it has been brought to that position. One of the reasons why the teaching even of science so often lacks the freshness and charm which men like Faraday and Hugh Miller could give it, is, I am disposed to think, that the teacher from the very first has known the science only in its latest phase. And the feverish hurry with which we all now hasten to acquaint ourselves with the newest thing leads to a neglect of the history of knowledge, a neglect which is both un-philosophical in itself and mischievous in its effects. In this respect, we English contrast very unfavourably with the Germans, who appear to have escaped the contempt, or at least indifference, for the history of knowledge which has made its mark on us.

It is a favourite commonplace with those who boast of the enormous strides knowledge has made in these latter days to say that even a schoolboy now would be able to puzzle Aristotle. Perhaps he would. Certainly Aristotle would very soon mightily puzzle him. To suppose that a boy, who is told in a moment the answer to a question which engaged the world for ages, is then and there as wise as he would have been if he had first felt the pressure of the question and been intellectually hungry for the answer, is as absurd as to suppose that a stake driven into the ground will stand as firmly as a tree that has grown and rooted on the spot. As a child cannot begin to talk like a philosopher, neither can he begin to see and think like one. *His* knowledge must have its childhood as well as that of the race. To the uninitiated, the acids and alkalies, air and water are very much what they were in the days of Priestley and Lavoisier; and the structure of the hills and valleys appear much as they appeared to Werner and Hutton rather than as they appear to the coming geologist, whose name has not yet got wind. But to the young *savant*, with his head full of original memoirs and his interest centred in the debateable outposts of his science, all this is otherwise. Such an one invites his pupils to come up higher, but does not see that his ladder has no rungs, no steps near the ground. Men like Davy and Faraday, on the other hand, who were largely self-taught, knew from their own experience how to connect the new with the old, knew how to preserve the continuity between everyday observation and scientific theory.

The chief educational value of science lies in its method; its dogmatic presentation renders it almost useless. The educator's problem in this case, then, should be so to supply the material of knowledge and so to direct his pupils in their mental manipulation of it as to awaken and foster the habits of mind by which new truths were discovered and new hypotheses tested. To do this, it is of the first importance to keep distinct the principles of the science and the evidence on which these rest. When a science is wrought into what the old logicians called a *doctrina*, the principles come first, and what is really the evidence is deduced from them, so that the original relation of the two is inverted; and a generalization, which is really grounded on a number of particulars, appears to prove them instead of being proved by them. This is what is usually meant by the synthetic or deductive method. Now, this more systematic arrangement certainly affords a much more complete command and oversight of the subject-matter. Such ideal arrangement is in fact the end at which we are to aim; the more a science allows us to use general propositions, the more perfect it is. But, on the other hand, the specially scientific training is lost on this method; nothing is learnt of the way in which general laws are established, but only of how they are applied.

Hence, a combination of the two methods seems to suggest itself. First, what the logicians call the analytic method, i.e. the method of discovery, so far as discovery is methodic, apart, therefore, from its fruitless and for beginners uninstructive deviations. According to this plan, then, we shall start from facts familiarly known, but not necessarily those from which the original investigator set out, although in the hands of an enthusiastic teacher these when skilfully handled can, if otherwise suitable, be made much more interesting. From such facts, so far as possible, the pupils should be able either themselves to detect, or at once to recognize, the general law. And I may add, by the way, that even when, as often happened, the original investigation did not proceed inductively but deductively, i.e. started from a hypothesis which was established by its consequences, it is none the less true that the inductive method is the best educationally at the outset. But, when, in this manner, one or two of the leading principles of the science have been reached and appear to the young student to have some flesh and blood and life about them, when he is in no danger of taking them on authority, or remaining oblivious of the ground on which they rest, then the smoother and more potent synthetic method may be adopted. Even now, however, as little as possible in its dogmatic dress, but wherever possible as what the logicians call the genetic method, a longer but educationally a more valuable procedure—in plainer words, the applications of the general principle are to be reached by working a series of problems. The advance to new and more complicated principles will call for a fresh resort to the analytic method; and so on continually.

The proportions in which the two methods will be employed will necessarily vary with the science and to some extent too with the stage at which it is studied. But, educationally, those sciences are best which afford full opportunities for both methods. And foremost amongst these I should place experimental physics. Chemistry, on the other hand, is certainly of little value as a mental training for the young; because, notwithstanding the entertainment it affords and the interest it awakens, the thinking required is either very easy and mechanical, little more than remembering analysis tables, or it is very difficult—quite beyond the power of a schoolboy—and moreover requiring extensive knowledge of facts, and being into the bargain largely hypothetical. As Archdeacon Wilson, formerly Headmaster of Clifton College, well said: "The notions of force, cause, composition of causes, are too abstruse in this subject for boys to get any hold of them. Hence it is, as a matter of fact, accepted as a mass of authoritative dogmas. ...It is of all subjects the most liable to cram, and the most useless as a branch of training when crammed."

The difference between certainty and probability or conjecture, between truth and opinion, is one which the educator should not fail to make felt. It is not of course desirable that subjects which are still mainly in the hypothetical stage should be taught in schools and to beginners. But what is merely probable or supposable, or matter of opinion, so far exceeds in quantity what is certain, that we cannot go far in any direction without coming upon it. Nor, if matters of probability and opinion could be wholly excluded from the scholar's attention, is it desirable that they should be. To keep him in an atmosphere of real or apparent certainty, when in after life three-quarters of his intellectual occupation will be to deal with uncertainties, is as foolish as it would be to keep him out of the water till he has learnt to swim. It is one of the most serious objections—and, so far as I can see, almost a fatal objection—to mathematical training, that it deals so exclusively with matters of demonstration in which there is no room for doubt, and, therefore, no exercise in the balancing of probabilities, a study, which, as Huxley said, "knows nothing of observation, nothing of induction, nothing of experiment, nothing of causation." Of course, the whole point of this remark bears against the *exclusive* study of mathematics; as furnishing a training in connected thinking, in formal exactness, mathematics are invaluable.

To know that you do not know is also knowledge; and, perhaps, there is no knowledge a man can possess that will do more to save him from error than a clear perception of his ignorance, of the line at which certainty ceases and doubt begins. To know this well is the first step towards suspension of judgment and deliberation. He who has but vague ideas of proof, who knows nothing clearly and distinctly, or he who has taken his knowledge on trust, cannot distinguish the certain from the uncertain, the obscure and the doubtful from the self-evident and demonstrative, opinion and prejudice from truth and knowledge. We see here again, then, that no efforts should be spared to make the young mind intellectually exacting; and, where certainty is not forthcoming, proportioning its conditional assent to the evidence. But this is much more than an intellectual matter. To know what truth is, to have a feeling for proof, is necessary but not sufficient. Descartes used to maintain that the will as well as the understanding is concerned in judging and that it is to the will's share in the process that error is due. Perhaps there is not much more in this than in the common adage "the wish is father to the thought"; but, at any rate, Descartes' exposition of it is worth our notice. Our understanding he says is limited: there are many things of which we can form no clear idea, many of which our ideas are obscure and indistinct. In such cases, the form of a judgment is necessarily presented to us—as, for example, in the moot questions whether the world had a beginning in time or whether matter is infinitely divisible. Here I have, let it be supposed, no clear idea; yet, none the less, in thinking about it, the two contradictory judgments, the world had, or had not, a beginning, matter is, or is not, infinitely divisible, present themselves to my understanding. Now, there are but two ways to avoid error: first to know absolutely and perfectly what is true, and secondly, in the case of ignorance, to know clearly that I do not know and to refrain from deciding. The latter is my only alternative here, and so long as I refrain from affirming either of the possible propositions, I am only ignorant but not in error. And this no doubt would be my position if intellect were alone concerned; but then the will comes in. And the will, unlike the intellect, has no limits: it embraces everything, the unknown equally with the known: where the intellect is indifferent, the will has a choice and affirms or denies accordingly. Descartes' motive in all this was theological. He was concerned to shew that error is due to man's volition and could not be charged upon God. Man's ignorance as distinct from man's error did not give Descartes much trouble; because he could easily shew, at least to his own satisfaction, that the imperfection of a part taken alone—and ignorance is only imperfection—is quite compatible with the perfection of the universe as a whole. Though largely a piece of special pleading, Descartes' doctrine is psychologically sound. As I remarked at the beginning of this lecture, there are some truths we cannot pervert, however anxious we may be; but, so far as our power to determine the movements of our ideational mechanism reaches, so far we have the power to deceive and cheat ourselves, and this is the case in the whole region of probability. If our interests incline us to one side, then, unless our love of truth is superior to them, and the less we have acquired a logical cast of mind, the more certainly shall we concentrate our attention on the *pros* and thereby exclude the *cons*, or on the *cons* and exclude the *pros*, as the case may be. Not merely so, but it is one of the effects of this emotional preference to heighten the intensity of such ideas as are allowed to occupy consciousness. How great this intensity may be we can see in the illusions sometimes consequent on strong desire. The upshot is clear. The materials for a definite judgment are unneutralized by opposing appearances and we judge and act accordingly. When bewitched into loving Bottom, Titania said:

> *Come sit thee down upon this flowery bed,*
> *While I thy amiable cheeks do coy,*
> *And stick musk roses in thy sleek smooth head,*
> *And kiss thy fair large ears, my gentle joy;*

yet, by and by, her eyes were opened, and she exclaimed:

> *O! how mine eyes do loathe his visage now.*

But so fortunate a *finale* is by no means general when once we have deceived ourselves into a false decision. The opposing reasons have been scattered and banished, the concurring reasons have become consolidated into a mental concept, perhaps have received a favourable name, and thickly there concretes around them a mass of error and prejudice, having the semblance of truth, because shielded from all that can expose or refute it. Nevertheless, that very word 'prejudice' which I have just used and its troop of synonyms, 'prepossession,' 'preconception,' 'bias,' 'one-sidedness,' 'obliquity of judgment,' and the like wake one up to the fact that without the help of psychological exposition the world is well enough aware of the chief source of error.

And yet, is it well enough aware? Are parents and schoolteachers well enough aware? That a man is more liable to error the less he is "inured to reflection and the handling of evidence," the less he has learnt to require and to submit to proof; that, above all, he is more liable to error the less a love of truth is paramount in him and the more he is swayed by his own interests and feelings—all this is as trite and commonplace as it would be to say that bread is the staff of life. The unfortunate difference, however, is that we live up to the one truth so much better than to the other. If action is the measure of conviction, then I doubt if educators are adequately convinced on this point. But I am not going to be guilty of the impertinence of exhorting you to be more urgent in this than your predecessors; and that, not because I do not feel strongly myself, but because I should be unwilling to believe that you do not feel as much. It is a question not of the will but of the way, that concerns us; and, as to that, I can only summarize what I have already said.

In the first place, I would urge that, from the outset, the pupil should learn as little as possible on authority and shape his ideas as far as possible for himself, his activity being directed but not superseded. It is on this ground chiefly that I urge an early training in observation and simple mathematics, and doubt the propriety of crowding out such lessons in order to make the most of the greater retentiveness of early years to impress paradigms and vocabularies, in all of which the scholar has to depend on his teacher, and has less scope for intellectual exercise. However, no doubt, there is time for both, if the literary teacher is not too greedy. At any rate, it is true, as Descartes—whose greatest service to mankind has been to teach them to doubt well—clearly saw, that the habit of receiving knowledge and opinions on authority during childhood and youth becomes in manhood so confirmed that an average man thus treated has almost lost the power to think independently.

In the second place, when the scholar comes to deal with general and abstract terms he should make clear and distinct to himself in what sense he uses them. For without clear conceptions it is impossible to have clear judgment: the mechanism of thought being bad, the work performed must be defective.

In the third place, his judgment should be exacting, and, where certainty is not forthcoming, should proportion its conditional assent to the evidence, answering to evidence as a ship does to her helm, and to nothing but the evidence. Long and careful training will be required to secure an ideal so soon stated in words. To attain this end, as well as on account of the preceding considerations, it is every way desirable, if not necessary, that the teacher should be acquainted with logic. True, men think correctly without logic, but they think more correctly with it. As Mill well says, " where there is a right way and a wrong way, there must be a difference between them and it must be possible to find out what the difference is "; and, when found out and expressed in words, it is a rule for the operation. If anyone is inclined to disparage rules, I say to him, try to learn anything for which there are rules, without knowing the rules, and see how you succeed. And, as part of a liberal education, I even think that logic should not be confined to the teacher. The exorbitant pretentions of the earlier logicians and the foolish disputations they encouraged have brought logic into undeserved contempt. No doubt, it requires to be taught with discretion and not by a logical pedant; but, well taught, it affords training by exercises and problems, as Professor Jevons has shewn, quite as valuable as the training afforded by mathematics, and a very desirable supplement to the latter.

But, over and above logical training, a profound love for truth must be quickened and kept vigorous in the student's mind. This is the crown and glory of an intellectual education, and to produce it is the sublimest office the teacher has to discharge. And here, as in so many other things, his example will be more effective than his precepts. There is nothing harder than to be at once enthusiastic and exact, free alike from the rigid uniformity of a calculating machine and the indiscriminating fervour of a partisan. Yet between these lies safety.

LECTURE VIII

EDUCATION VALUES

The idea which the term 'education values' is meant to convey is to be found as far back as Plato's exposition in the second and third books of the *Republic* of the respective functions of music and gymnastic. Again, after a wide interval, we meet it still more explicitly, though yet without a name, in Bacon's essay "Of Studies." Perhaps I may be allowed to indulge in a quotation from the latter: "*Histories* make Men Wise; *Poets*, Witty; the *Mathematicks*, subtile; *Naturall Philosophy*, deepe; *Morall*, grave; *Logick* and *Rhetorick*, Able to Contend.... Nay, there is no Stond or Impediment in the Wit, but may be wrought out by Fit *Studies*. Like as Diseases of the Body may have Appropriate Exercises.... Shooting is [good for] the Lungs and Breast; Gentle Walking for the Stomacke; Riding for the Head; and the like. So, if a Mans Wit be Wandering, let him *Study* the *Mathematicks*.... If his Wit be not Apt to distinguish or find differences, let him *Study* the Schoole-men. If he be not Apt to beat over Matters, and to call up one thing to Prove and Illustrate another, let him *Study* the *Lawyers' Cases*. So every defect of the Mind may have a Speciall Receit."

In Bain's *Education as a Science* we first come across the phrase 'education values,' and I think I may add that there, too, we have first any adequate discussion of the thing. A threefold analogy seems to underlie the phrase. Studies may be regarded as exercises, as medicines, or as foods. The first two are, more or less, combined in the passage from Bacon; perhaps it is the last that the use of the word 'values' most directly suggests. Physiological text-books have familiarized us with tables exhibiting the respective values of fat and lean, sugar, starch, etc., for the sustenance of brain or muscle, for maintaining warmth, preventing fatigue, and so on. To make a perfect diet we must have so much proteids, so much fat, and so much starch: if we live on bread alone, to get enough of the first of these we must take a great deal too much of the last; if we feed wholly on meat, we must take a large excess of the first to get the requisite equivalents of the others.

And, nowadays, all this is supposed to have some sort of application to the mind: to grow healthily, the mind must be appropriately fed; to develop to the utmost, it must have varied exercise; its specific defects must be met by specific remedies. So it comes that we are led to investigate mental dietetics, mental gymnastics, and mental therapeutics.

In entering upon an inquiry of this sort, it scarcely needs to be premised that we are only concerned with liberal education: how much mathematics the engineer must have or how many modern languages are required for a diplomatist—with such practical questions we have nothing to do. But there is still a narrower sense in which, at the outset at any rate, such an inquiry cannot be practical: we cannot straightway settle the several classes and forms of a secondary school, and the time-tables for each, according to the renovated curriculum. It will be well if we can get nearer to clear theoretical views on the subject as a whole.

But first, and just for a moment, let us return to the old question: what do we intend by education? The scholastic body in this country seems generally to have no answer ready on this question: it has, so to speak, not yet attained, though it is fast attaining, to an educational self-consciousness. We should have to gather an answer for ourselves by looking at the present position of our great schools, and at their past history. Their model is the scholar and gentleman. Such knowledge, or rather such learning, whether intrinsically useful or not, as is actually held in repute they seek to impart, though, from their slavish adherence to tradition, they rather lag behind than lead public opinion in this respect. Thus, the introduction of the so-called 'modern side,' and the increased attention given to science, modern languages, and history is, I venture to think, not the result of reflexion on the problem of education values, but simply a consequence of outside pressure. Educational theorists, on the other hand, are ready with exact answers, scientifically deduced, as to the end aimed at and the means to be employed. Yet the exactness is mainly formal. Without 'middle principles' (*axiomata media*) such theories can scarcely be brought effectively to bear on existing practice—least of all in a conservative country like ours, and with a very conservative class like the majority of English headmasters. Such as they are, however, the answers of the theorists run briefly as follows: Education is essentially the conscious direction by mature persons of the growth and development of the young. The aim is efficiency for the highest life. The individual must be fitted for, without being sacrificed to, the society of which he is to become not merely a member, but a unit. As to the process of education, it must consist mainly in exercise, and not in mere instruction. Such exercise, to be effective, must be sustained by a direct and not by a merely factitious interest. The education value of studies and their order—in fact, the pedagogic method generally—is to be ascertained from psychology.

Setting out from this ideal standpoint, it will be convenient, before coming to details, to notice, first, two matters of more general interest: the claims of society and the claims of the individual. Both of these bear directly and fundamentally on our inquiry as to the place and relative worth of various studies. Now, albeit that not too partial critic, the enlightened foreigner, is forward to allow that we are a philanthropic and public-spirited people, yet I think it must be owned that we are so, for the most part, in spite of our school curriculum. No doubt our playgrounds powerfully promote manliness and loyalty; but they do nothing to enlighten, and still less to expand, this youthful zeal to do and suffer for common ends. It will, I assume, be granted at once that the welfare, even the existence, of a free country depends upon the possession by its several members of sound knowledge, and the power to think soundly on social and political affairs. No matter what the individual's calling may be, no matter what his private bent, his country expects him to be fit to do his duty as one of the commonwealth. This claim, which has always been important, is more imperious than ever now. I do not need to dilate on this; if any man doubt of it, let him but look abroad and think. The difference between a collection of human beings, each of whom is only fitted and only disposed to make the most of himself and a community not more gifted or better equipped for individual ends, but with every member able and ready to co-operate for the good of the whole, is profound and absolute. It is comparable only with the gulf that separates, in the evolution of organic life, a few millions of infusoria from the man whose myriad cells are all co-operant and consentient parts of one living whole. And as is this difference, such, from the point of view of society, is the educational value of whatever can be done to fit the young for their future political and social life.

It would carry us quite beyond the limits of our subject to inquire at all precisely what means and material are forthcoming to this end. But I cannot forbear expressing surprise that a matter of such moment has received apparently so little attention amongst

us. Among Germans the culture of *Vaterlandsliebe* is a standing
theme; the mother-tongue, literature, history, and geography, are
all to be handled with this end kept steadily in sight. No doubt
much may be done in this way, and the work begun early; and,
when the teacher is awake to the importance of civic training,
much is done. Yet we want more. In the upper forms, economics
and political science should be regularly taught. Milton, in his
little Tractate, briefly but pointedly insists on the "Study of
Politicks; to know the beginning, end, and reasons of Political
Societies; that they [the students] may not be such poor, shaken,
uncertain Reeds, as many of our great Counsellers have lately
shown themselves, but steadfast pillars of the State." Let me
clench what I have to say on this point by a word from Professor
Seeley, and then pass on: "Any one who knows how much study
it takes in the present complication of human affairs to arrive at
solid political convictions, and how much taste for study there is
in the ordinary Englishman, whether he belongs to the class of
politicians or not, will arrive at the conclusion that our politicians
must be insufficiently educated, from the mere fact that political
science is so little taught in schools and colleges. An Englishman
often extends in after-life his knowledge of the subjects to which
he has been introduced at school or college, but does not very often
travel into quite new regions of knowledge....In these days, when
we are all more alive than our fathers were to the difficulty of the
science of government, I may venture, perhaps, to make the assertion that we shall never have a supply of competent politicians
until political science—i.e. roughly political economy and history
together—is made a prominent part of higher education[1]."

And now we come to the other topic of more general interest
that the educational ideal suggests, one which is the exact counterpart of the last—I mean the claims of individuality. To the
renovated curriculum, based on a psychological determination of
education values, it is objected that it is fitted for no one in
particular, and wholly disregards individual differences—just as
psychology deals with mind in general, and not with individual
minds. To put it briefly: What is best for all (collectively) is best for
none (individually). As there is, I suppose, no way of avoiding this
objection, it will be convenient to anticipate it, and to attempt to
clear the ground by a brief consideration of one or two general
points.

[1] Seeley, *Lectures and Essays*, p. 305.

We are often reminded how little school did for Newton and Darwin and other men of genius, and, though geniuses are rare, they are important to the same degree. It is, therefore, a serious objection if a curriculum, adapted for minds in general, fails to do justice to minds of a new and original type, or if the inevitable tendency of striving to secure a harmonious and many-sided development is to repress individuality and stereotype a mediocre caricature of the ideal man. The fact is, however, that there is nowadays an opposite danger, which is, if anything, more serious, namely, early and excessive specialization. In this the individual is apt to be sacrificed to the community. The public demand is for people who can do one thing well, and, following in the wake of this demand, our schools and universities encourage one-sided excellence—or, I would rather say, one-sidedness—by means of prizes and emoluments. I hesitate to use the phrase 'one-sided *excellence*,' because it is not the best man who suffers so much as the man of one talent. The very facility that characterizes genius, together with its eagerness, usually ensures time for more than one thing and an interest in many: so that frequently where there is absolute excellence, so to say, in one direction, there is also very creditable acquisition and efficiency in others. My experience as a teacher and an examiner would certainly lead me to say that the best at one thing are often best at several, or, at all events, good all round; and, equally, that the worst at one are often poor all round: your 'wooden spoon' is generally wooden all through. Perhaps nothing can be done for *him*; but the second-class man who contrives, by neglecting everything else, to be ranked as just respectable in some special department of knowledge or practice is to be pitied and may be helped. If we could follow his career, we should probably find that this mediocre specialist is worse off in the end, even in his narrow department, than he would have been if he had attended more to what is called general culture. The long and short of it, then, seems to be that the first claim of individuality, when by this we understand a one-sided bent, is to be saved from itself, so to speak. The ablest specialist already has varied interests, and we have but to provide for them; the common-place specialist needs, even for the sake of his speciality, and still more for his own sake, to have such varied interests awakened and maintained.

Of course, if provision is made *only* for his general humanity and not for what makes him *hic* or *ille*, not for his *haecceity* as the schoolmen used to say, a man will have cause to complain. We had a Fellow in Trinity, who, as often as he had the chance to order dinner, always ordered spitchcocked eels, and as his position in the college gave him the opportunity of securing his favourite dish not unfrequently, he shewed at other times quite a due relish for beef and mutton. Now, what Shrewsbury and Cambridge failed to do for Darwin was to furnish him with his spitchcocked eels, even as a *hors d'œuvre*. But we must not, from this and similar cases, argue that future Darwins are to have only, or will even only want, their *Lieblingsspeise*, as the Germans say. To meet the inevitable difficulty referred to first, that a curriculum generally adapted to everybody will be precisely adapted to none, and may therefore tend to starve originality, the chief requisites seem to be (*a*) some amount of elasticity in the curriculum, (*b*) some leisure for work outside it.

On this last point a word. I am satisfied that at the universities men are over-lectured, over-coached; have their time and reading too much mapped out for them. The evils due to the prevailing specialization are thereby aggravated: a man runs in harness along a prescribed road till he becomes dazed and helpless when relieved of the bit and blinkers. Assuming good preliminary training, I should say that from the sixteenth year onwards most pupils would gain by tasting the sweets of liberty in connexion with work, if that be not a too palpable contradiction in terms. Something should be expected of them outside the prescribed course. Sometimes they might choose to do more than the regulation minimum in an old direction; oftener, perhaps, they might prefer to break quite new ground.

To sum up on these two preliminary questions. As every pupil must look forward to being not only a man but a citizen, the training and knowledge requisite for the efficient discharge of social and political functions must form part of his education, and have a place and attention proportionate to its obvious importance. This is soon said. It seems true; but to carry it out would involve very considerable changes in the prevailing curriculum. Again, as every human being is in some sort *sui generis*, two opposite needs arise. On the one hand, care must be taken lest society, according to its inevitable tendency to encourage division of labour, does not exploit these individual peculiarities merely for its own ends, and in particular that it does not begin to exploit them too soon. The motto of the old Mechanics' Institutes must not be forgotten: to make a man a better mechanic we must make the mechanic a better man. On the other hand, each individual should have help and opportunity, either at home or at school, to exult in what is his peculiar strength, and, being thus satisfied instead of being starved, he will be more likely to be interested and diligent in other ways.

And now at length we come to the main question of education values in relation to school-work generally. This is a subject upon which it is thought that the psychologist and the logician may throw some light, and there are writers on educational theory who profess to deduce their entire deliverances from psychological first principles. Unhappily, the psychology from which they set out is none of the best. One is constantly coming across disquisitions on the training of the senses, the training of the memory, the training of the imagination; of the faculties of conception, abstraction, judgment, and so on. I know that many most excellent precepts are given to the world in this way: I admit that it has the merit of being popular and seeming easy. But I dare to say, and that confidently, that it is a bad way none the less, one that psychologists, who keep their science and its applications distinct, rarely follow, and against which they frequently protest[1]. It is humiliating to reflect that this defunct doctrine of faculties, having first retarded the progress of psychology itself, should now be revived to darken knowledge under the guise of psychology applied to education.

The first thing the educationist should be clear about is as to what he intends, as to what his end and aim is, or rather should be. To ascertain this ideal, he must turn not to psychology, but to life: it is a social and ethical, rather than a psychological, problem. So regarded, it would never occur to anyone to say that the end of education is to train the senses, to train the memory, to train the imagination, and so forth. You might do all these things, as certain 'practical' psychologists advise, and have a very sorry specimen of humanity as the result. Even if these faculties were not the mere abstractions they are, it would still be little better than attempting to grow a tree upside down to start from them. Psychology, as a science, may be said to fall into two parts: an analytic part, and a synthetic or genetic part. It is this last that is mainly of importance to the educationist: if, instead of attending to this, he attempts to make piecemeal applications of psychological analysis, he is in

[1] Cf. Bain, *Education as a Science*, pp. 122 and 125.

great danger of bewildering himself and of discrediting a good cause. But the misfortune is that psychology is most complete in its analytic part; and, just where the educationist wants it most, it fails him most. Still, as his business is to direct the growth and development of mind, what is scientifically known concerning the laws and order of mental growth and development is deserving of his first attention.

When we ask, then, about the education value of a subject, the answer will depend altogether upon the stage at which it is proposed to teach it. There are some, no doubt, ready to affirm that the collective experience of school-teachers has long since attained to the truth in this matter without waiting for the pompous parade of scientific deduction. So much, or rather so little—for it is a very simple matter—might have been expected, certainly. Yet, alas! the order of study, as commonly pursued, was till recently as unscientific—or, if you prefer it, as unnatural—as it well could be. To be sure, theory and practice are coming into accord now as fast perhaps as the *vis inertiae* of human institutions will allow. But there are still a good many schools, I suspect, in which grammar lessons are given long before the age of ten, in which Latin precedes French, in which irregularities of accidence are learnt in wholesale batches before any *copia verborum*, or any acquaintance with sentence construction, is secured at all; many schools, again, in which the multiplication-tables are repeated *en bloc* before they have been verified or understood in detail, in which geometry begins with Euclid's *Elements*, and the teaching of chemistry with a lesson on oxygen. After all, it does *not* seem to be so very obvious how widely the natural order of acquisition differs from the logical order of exposition; and perhaps it is one of the evils we owe to the existence of books that they tend to hide this difference. The education value of a study depends not only on the stage at which it is taught, but also on the mode and order in which it is presented. This, however, is a new point, to which I will return presently.

There is another evil casually noticed a moment ago, to which it may be worth while to refer first, and this is an evil which is, perhaps, partly attributable to the absence of books—I mean the practice of learning by rote. This practice has had much to do with dislocating the natural order of studies, and particularly so with grammar and language, religious formulæ, and the like. For lists and formal statements can be learnt by heart long before they can be understood; they may be 'committed to memory' as to a sort of mental crop for use in days to come. I am surprised to find Professor Bain countenancing this view. He says: "For the years between six and ten very little can be done that involves severe processes of the reason; and yet the mind is highly plastic and susceptible; so that presumably this is the age of the maximum of pure memory as typified by language-acquisitions, not merely vocables and their connexions with things, but connected compositions, as stories, hymns, and the expressed forms of knowledge[1]." Precisely what is meant by this last phrase is not very clear, but there can be little doubt that it would cover the practice of committing to memory facts and formulæ that cannot for some time be understood. It is quite a question whether the most indelible impressions *are* made between the ages of six and ten, unless by a disproportionate expenditure of effort. No doubt *imitativeness* is a special feature of childhood at this time, and the fact can, of course, be turned to account in many ways. But this natural imitativeness does not trammel the juvenile mind, or repress its spontaneity as the *propria quae maribus, as in presenti,* or other gerund-grinding devices must tend to do. It is nothing better than a grim joke to tell us that the child's mind is 'highly susceptible' to torture of this kind. A vast amount of harm has, I fear, been wrought by habituating the young at the outset to this unnatural use of what is called their memory; and for this there is no denying that the old 'faculty psychology' is very largely to blame.

To return to the point just now left aside, even if taught at the proper stage, the education value of a study will depend almost entirely upon the mode in which it is handled, and the order in which its several parts are presented. Thus boldly stated, this proposition is ridiculously obvious, but it covers a number of particulars which have been frequently overlooked. And after all, what is less noticed than just what is too familiar for notice?

To begin, then, the natural order of acquisition differs widely from the logical order of exposition. Each successive presentation of an advancing science clears away some of the scaffolding by which the science has been built up, and thereby renders it simpler and compacter from within, but possibly much less accessible from without. To this continuous condensation or compression of knowledge there is no assignable limit. But much that is thus extruded

[1] Bain, *Education as a Science,* pp. 186–7.

as of only antiquarian interest will often be found to be educationally of the highest value—assuming, of course, that it is reasonable to expect the order in which the individual can best appropriate knowledge to resemble, at any rate broadly, the order in which the human race at first ascertained and excogitated it. The untrained teacher—the teacher, that is, who knows his subject, but has yet to learn how to use it as a means of education—is very apt to begin with the expository order, at least an outline, perhaps has to use a text-book so arranged by a writer who is alike ignorant and unconcerned about education. Reverting to one of the analogies which we have seen to be implied in the phrase 'education value,' we are reminded that a given article of diet is entirely altered in its physiological effects by varying its concentration and the form in which it is administered—as with beef-extract, roast beef and bouillon, for instance. So it is with studies and their effect upon the minds of the young. Many are the instances of the old fallacy of arguing *a dicto simpliciter ad dictum secundum quid*, or the converse, which we may find among the educational advocates of certain studies, particularly among writers who, like Herbert Spencer, press the claims of science in season and out of season. The late Frank Buckland, I believe it was, who used to maintain that there was nothing to beat a crocodile-chop as a breakfast dish; but, then, he was careful to add that it must be cooked properly. To make a slice of crocodile at once palatable and wholesome is, we may be sure, no easy matter. Neither is it an easy matter to make natural science a generally efficient means of intellectual discipline. This is, in fact, the hardest thing to do with it: there are two other things, both very good, which may much more easily be done with it. It may be imparted as useful information, and I am far from intending that this is not worth doing. Or, again, the wonders and the romance of science may serve as an important element of culture: this also is excellent, and well worth doing. But when the place of science in the school curriculum is discussed, it is surely vital to know which of these three qualifications is intended: is it to be practical, cultural, or disciplinary?

If the first alone is intended, probably the man who has learnt science can teach it, and a reasonably good text-book of the requisite dimensions may be found ready to hand. The second will make less demands on the teacher's scientific knowledge, but will require some feeling and imagination, some literary training and rhetorical skill; here, too, writers like Humboldt, Tyndall, Huxley, and Wallace will provide him with ample printed material. But, to make science a means of mental discipline, a knowledge of the subject is only half the battle; a knowledge of its history is hardly less important, and a really helpful text-book will be far harder to find.

Another subject, the educational properties and worth of which vary most strikingly with the mode in which it is served up, is Mathematics. In the years 1883 and 1885 Professors Henrici and Chrystal made the teaching of mathematics the topic of sectional addresses at the British Association meetings of those years. These encourage me to say what I should have no title to say on my own account. Even in the address of the year 1889 by Dr Glaisher there are two sentences so appropriate to what I am intending, that I may fairly quote them. "The whole science," says Dr Glaisher, "suffers from want of avenues of approach, and many beautiful branches of mathematics are regarded as difficult and technical merely because they are not easily accessible." Later on he adds: "In any treatise or higher text-book it is always desirable that references to the original memoirs should be given, and, if possible, short historical notices also. I am sure that no subject loses more than mathematics by any attempt to dissociate it from its history." These remarks refer, no doubt, to the higher branches of mathematics, but, from the point of view of the beginner, are perhaps as true of the lower. The world had probably worn out many an abacus before it constructed the multiplication-table; even the deductive geometry of Euclid was led up to by an age of inductive geometry among the Egyptians. Now, what I am venturing to maintain is that the individual should grow his own mathematics, just as the race has had to do. But I do not propose that he should grow it as if the race had not grown it too. When, however, we set before him mathematics, be it high or low, in its latest and most generalized and most compacted form, we are trying to manufacture a mathematician, not to grow one[1].

To the uninitiated onlooker it must seem an odd instance of the waywardness of things human that, while in subjects like arithmetic, algebra, and trigonometry the latest expositions are preferred, and all traces of history swept away, in geometry—with us in England, that is to say—Euclid's *Elements* are still allowed to stand. This certainly looks like erring in the opposite extreme, and Professor Henrici evidently thinks so. "The chief progress in

[1] Cp. *supra*, p. 88.

geometrical teaching," he says, "has to be sought in the introduction of modern ideas and methods into the very elements, and
modern teaching ought to take full account of this"; and he quotes
no less an authority than Professor Sylvester as urging with characteristic warmth that Euclid should "be honourably shelved or
buried 'deeper than did ever plummet sound' out of the schoolboy's reach." Why isn't it done? The practical difficulties, largely
depending on examinations, like so many other practical difficulties,
do not now concern us. But a plea for the retention of Euclid is
sometimes made on the theoretical ground that Euclid's *Elements*
are a logical training. I gather that Professor Henrici attaches
some weight to this, and he suggests that reforms might be facili-
tated "by introducing some of the elements of logic into the teaching
of language." I certainly should not myself allow the plea, if we
may digress to consider this point for a moment. If Euclid's
Elements served so well to exemplify logical principles and precepts, we should expect logicians to resort to them as a generally
accessible repertory of logical instances. Yet we find nothing of the
kind. The most severe strictures I know on the method of Euclid
were made by two mathematicians who were also logicians: I mean
Arnauld and Pierre Nicole, the authors of the Port Royal Logic.
Direct logical training must surely be of the highest value educationally; but there is no adequate substitute for it. In particular,
on those parts of logic which are of most importance educationally—
as, e.g. the doctrines of definition, division, the conversion and
opposition of propositions, formal fallacies, and the whole theory
of induction, hypothesis and analogy—Euclid's *Elements* do not even
incidentally throw light. Moreover, a great deal of geometrical
knowledge rests upon direct intuition of the spatial relations
concerned, and this kind of evidence can be appreciated some
time before the cogency of a train of reasoning can be duly
felt. When that later stage is reached, a complete logical training
is desirable. Hence there arises the dilemma: either the geometry
is deferred for the sake of the logic, or the logic stinted by means
of the geometry.

But we must return to the general question of the educational
treatment of mathematics, on which I have still a word to say.
I take my text this time from Professor Chrystal. Speaking of
algebra, he says: "The whole training consists in example-grinding.
What should have been merely the help to attain the end has
become the end itself. The result is that algebra, as we teach it, is

neither an art nor a science, but an ill-digested farrago of rules, whose object is the solution of examination problems." This is strong language from the writer of a great book on algebra: perhaps it is too strong. In schools, at any rate, it must be allowed that the solution of problems affords an admirable, though one-sided, mental training. Yet, it is far from an objection to a study that its educational efficacy is restricted and specific, provided we do not expect more of it than it can do. I am told, however, that this example-grinding must be persevered in, in order that the student may attain due facility in the use of notations and devices. This line of defence seems to point to a defect. To the boy who goes right through this grind the drill may do some good, and such a one is likely to be a mathematical specialist. But what to the boy who does not go through with it, whose speciality is not mathematics? It is as if, having only the means to build myself a cottage, I expend it all in building what would be an excellent porch to a castle; or, having only half-an-hour in which to make a sketch, I give all the time to a five-barred gate in the foreground. If intentional, it looks like the sacrifice of proportion to a mistaken idea of thoroughness; but it is probably not intentional, it is probably the unforeseen outcome of circumstances. Mathematical text-books have been usually written by mathematicians, not by educationists; and they have usually mathematics and not education as their shaping idea—in a word, the writers are usually professionals, and their aim is primarily professional. Now, the question I would ask is this: Would not the general education value of mathematics be increased if some of the pains taken to ensure expertness of manipulation were directed to ensuring rather more insight, and something of a general survey of mathematics as a system? It is surely often better to have an outline-map of a whole country rather than a piece of the Ordnance Survey of the same size as the map. This, I take it, is what Professor Chrystal is fighting for when he denounces the practice of "retarding their [the students'] progress by making the details and illustrations of particular rules and methods ends in themselves."

But there is still a subject, the extreme importance of which calls for much fuller notice than there is now time for. I mean language and literature, the studies graced with the proud title of the "Humanities." Here, again, the issue as to the place and worth of these studies is confused, spite of much discussion, for want of exact distinctions. It is as if we had to ascertain the dietetic value of plum-pudding, and one argued from an analysis of the flour, another from an analysis of the suet, and another from that of the plums, or perhaps the plum-stones; or as if, in discussing the good of dancing, one should argue from the muscular exertion, another from the nervous excitement. There seem to be three things, at any rate, never actually separated in this department of school-work, which must be estimated strictly apart before many of the vexed questions as to its value can be dealt with rationally. They are grammar (or, more generally, philology), translation and com-position or linguistic training, and literature.

It is the neglect or the refusal to estimate these elements sepa-rately that gives the advocates of the old classical training much of their apparent advantage. Nobody denies the unique excellence of Greek literature or the cultural value of Greek and Roman history. But just in proportion to the beauty and sublimity of the thought and sentiments, just in proportion to the grandeur and heroism of the incidents, must be their relative independence of their original dress. For no one, surely, will confound the necessary dependence of thought on language with a necessary dependence on one particular language. In art generally, the medium of ex-pression is comparatively accidental to the form expressed. The beauty of the Venus of Milo, or of the Laocoon, is not greatly diminished by reproduction in bronze. It would be quite worth while to have a careful discussion of this very point as regards Greek literature, the case being argued on some selected pieces of trans-lation by some acknowledged master, like Professor Jebb. Let us suppose that the loss in effect is comparable to the substitution of monochrome for colour, as we have it, for example, in passing from Raphael's finished pictures to some of his cartoons. Having got this far, let us put the practical question in this form: Is it more desirable that everybody shall be familiar with Raphael's master-pieces, in autotypes at any rate, or shall these be carefully withheld lest they should discredit an ancient practice of painting colour-diagrams in accordance with treatises on Raphael's chromatic combinations? In other words, shall we withhold the soul of classical literature expressed in English, lest it serve as a crib, and perhaps banish classical exercises?

Such a question leads us to look at the other element, and to ask whether Greek and Latin accidence and syntax have any specific educational value purely as a discipline, assuming, that is —as is avowedly the case—that the many who learn them do not, for one reason or other, obtain any appreciable culture from their literatures thereby. This, I feel, is a harder question to answer, but largely because, as a matter of fact, our whole apparatus for this kind of discipline has been elaborated in connexion with Latin and Greek. As the then Headmaster of Repton said, in his reply to the Cambridge Syndicate in 1880: "It will take a generation to formulate anything approaching to so correct a scheme in the case of French and German." Supposing it granted that no adequate substitute is at present to hand, it would still be advantageous to consider whether there is anything in the nature of things to prevent the same discipline being secured by other means. In the report of the Cambridge Syndicate to which I have just referred there is an admirable letter from Mr Arthur Sidgwick. The following sentences of his bear directly on our question: "I think there is no doubt that those boys who reach the highest forms in a school get advantage from Greek which it would be difficult to get from other studies except at a greater expense of time, if even so. *Accuracy*, detailed and sustained, is, no doubt, well promoted by many studies; but certainly a language with a complicated accidence can be made to promote it thoroughly. *Subtlety* of mind may be exercised by many studies, but by none more than a language which has a delicate and complex syntax capable of expressing fine shades of thought with precision—a language, too, which, by its reach of particles, to a real scholar can almost be said to give action and instruction. *The sense and judgment* are perhaps better trained by language than by anything (that can come into a school course); but of languages that would be most successful which is in idiom remote from the learner's vernacular, and in its literature most rich and varied."

Now, the stress that is here laid on complexity of accidence and syntax and on diversity of idiom seems to point to the unquestionable advantage of seeing the structure of thought exhibited in an unfamiliar dress; the pupil comes in this way to realize distinctly and easily what he could otherwise only attain by a very difficult process of reflexion. All this points primarily only to the advantage of having another language to hold the mirror to one's own. The special fitness of one foreign language over another for this particular purpose becomes then a question of degree, and compensating advantages of another kind would have a claim to consideration. Moreover, the faculty of reflecting on language being once quickened—say by French or German—can be turned and exercised upon our own. To deny this would be tantamount to saying that accuracy and precision of thought are only attainable by the man who thinks in Greek, which would be the old fallacy of identifying thought with a particular vehicle of expression, to which I just now referred. The mention of compensating advantages in other languages reminds me that later on in his letter Mr Sidgwick allows that half the boys who learn Greek at a public school get none of the higher advantages, while for the worst boys it is, he says, "not merely useless, but pernicious. The accidence is so much more complex than any other accidence they learn, that they *never master it*." I do not mention this for the sake of its immediate bearing on the burning question of compulsory Greek, but for the sake of an implication that it seems to contain affecting the educational value of Greek for anybody. In what sense is the hardness of Greek accidence, which is a positive evil to those who succumb under it, a positive good to those who triumph over it? Is it simply the general bracing that comes of vanquishing any difficulty; or if the expense in time were less— taking time as a measure of difficulty—would the gain from Greek be greater? In so far as the education value of a foreign language is to facilitate what I may, perhaps, call the objectification or projection of language as the vehicle of thought, that by this temporary estrangement it may afterwards be more effectually appropriated, so far the difficulties diminish its value instead of adding to it. Unless, indeed, it be maintained that the entire utility, so far as linguistic training is concerned, depends directly on complexity of accidence and syntax. But, if this were so, there are, I presume, other languages still more complex than Greek. It is, I am aware, but a very vague business attempting to apply quantitative notions to matters of this kind; still, I cannot forbear asking whether complexity and diversity beyond a certain degree do not defeat our end, which I am now assuming to be acquiring a mastery of language as a vehicle of thought, and by means of Greek grammar. For better for worse, with the development of the race, language has become less inflexional, our own especially, and who shall say it is for worse? It is a question, therefore, whether, after all, languages more akin to ours, such as German and French, are not enough to furnish a standard of comparison and the play of cross-lights, and yet not so strange as to entail either the sacrifice of English to literal translation, or the sacrifice of accuracy and subtlety to the demands of our vernacular.

It has been often urged—as, for example, by Bain—that the mixture of conflicting studies which the present classical curriculum involves, impedes the course of the learner. It seeks to give him at once "logical training, training in English, literary culture, general philology." Assuming, then, that we carefully distinguish these, and that Greek and Roman literature are not, as instruments of culture, inseparable from the Greek and Latin languages, it is a question whether, for merely grammatical training, Latin is not the best instrument; and whether, at any rate when the preliminary grammatical training has been secured, training in English will not be most effectually secured through English.

As to the logical training, again, one word—and here I am more upon my own ground. I feel sure that language-training, whether in ancient or modern languages, is no efficient substitute for logic. It is a better substitute than Euclid, certainly: it gives unconsciously what Mr Arthur Sidgwick happily calls "sense and judgment." But just as little as unconscious correctness of idiom will suffice in the matter of expression, so little will unconscious sagacity and intelligence suffice in the matter of discursive reasoning.

LECTURE IX

DEVELOPMENT OF WILL AND FORMATION
OF HABITS AND CHARACTER

We enter now upon an entirely new division of our subject, and, if it is difficult to formulate a theory of intellectual training, to formulate a theory of moral training is more difficult still. Human beings are in their tastes, dispositions and characters much more various than they are intellectually: intellectual differences are largely a difference of degree, but moral differences amount to differences of kind. Individuality counts for more here than it did there: almost every man now is *sui generis*. Besides this, the psychology of emotion and volition is much more complicated and obscure. I must forewarn you, therefore, not to expect much; and beg you besides to hold the subject answerable to some extent for the imperfect treatment it will receive at my hands. But the harder it is to cope with all the intricacies of moral character and conduct the more it behoves us to remember at the outset that we are still in the region of uniformity. Diverse as human tastes and actions are, when considered in relation to the individual, there are points in which they agree. All objects, no matter how various, are pleasurable or painful, interesting or uninteresting; and pleasure and pain tend to affect all alike, the one attracts, the other repels. Habits the most opposite grow up and grow stronger in the same general way, much as thorns or grapes, figs or thistles do. Wherever motives conflict, the general outlines of the conflict are identical, though all the details may be different. Deliberation and decision are the same things, whatever be the results to which they lead, and are not one jot the less uniform in their general features because the agent feels that if he would, he could decide differently.

And not only are there uniformities of great moment amid all the diversities of human conduct but there are as great, or even greater, uniformities in the growth of human character. When we think of the overwhelming diversity, the wonder rather is that the laws of moral activity and moral growth or deformity have not been more overlooked than that they should be understood by the mass of men so little. Still, all whose duty it is to train the young ought assuredly to spare no pains to gain a much deeper insight into these laws than the untutored light of nature will

afford them. One great reason, no doubt, why the rising generation at any time is so far from perfect is that the generation in
advance of it is itself so imperfect. But, after making all allowance
for this sufficiently humbling consideration, there remains a
tremendous residuum of mischief due solely to ignorance of the
conditions of moral growth and training.

Of all the mistakes made, perhaps the most serious and by no
means the rarest is to ignore the existence of any such thing as
conditions of moral growth at all. When a child warmly resents
a bump from the table by hitting the table in return, as if the table
knew better and could feel, people smile at such innocent simplicity;
but they little think that, in resenting some offence of the child's as
they would do if it were committed by one of themselves, they are
equally foolish though not so innocent. To fill his pockets with apples
or sugar candy, when nobody is looking, is of course a fault calling for
correction even in a youth of five; but to scold and castigate him with
the utmost severity, because theft in one legally responsible might
entail a month's imprisonment, is a piece of stupid blundering that
must tend to upset his moral balance altogether. Instead of having
a reason for avoiding a second offence, he has no motive except
that of unreasoning fear, and learns from such severity to dislike
not pilfering but only punishment. Conscience is not an innate
faculty independent of experience and culture; and a great deal
of the juvenile depravity about which ignorant persons talk so
much is no more depravity than unripeness is rottenness. "Many
a child," says Dr Carpenter, "is put into 'durance vile' for not
learning 'the little busy bee,' who simply *cannot* give its small
mind to the task, whilst disturbed by stern commands and threats
of yet severer punishment for a disobedience it cannot help[1]."
Here, again, the fact that the power of self-control is not inborn
but is of slow growth is ignored, and the further fact, too, that
emotional disturbance instead of increasing only diminishes this
power. The better to avoid all such mistakes and to see their
absurdity let us, then, study for a while the general characteristics
of our moral nature and the conditions of moral growth.

All human activity is broadly determined by, and ultimately rests
upon, the facts of pleasure and pain. Keenly as this statement
would be debated, when expressed in some forms, it is none the
less substantially admitted by everybody. There is nothing upon
which both in theory and practice there is more universal agreement.

[1] W. B. Carpenter, *Mental Physiology*, p. 135.

If no living thing, high or low, could be either pained or pleased, helped or hindered by a given action, there would be no motive either for doing it or leaving it undone. And if the same were true of all actions whatever, then all actions would be alike indifferent; there would be no right conduct and no wrong conduct, for conduct altogether would cease. We cannot conceive such a state; a life in which all alike was indifferent, whether bitter or sweet, beautiful or ugly, true or false, would be a life indistinguishable from the inertia and monotony of death or the impassiveness of a machine. Pleasure and pain are, then, the more fundamental notions even though the good and the right are practically the more important. And yet, because the words have ignoble and unworthy associations, and because from the standpoint of a particular individual, pleasure and duty often conflict, it is not unnatural that we should feel a certain repugnance to a statement which we are none the less unable to gainsay. But, as to the first difficulty, a little reflexion is enough to shew us that pleasures and pains are of many kinds. We do not despise the pleasures of art, of knowledge, of virtue, and yet these are just as truly pleasures as sensuous enjoyment or luxurious ease. And, again, though the right may not coincide with the pleasant for an individual and in a particular case, yet common sense assumes that they do coincide for society and on the whole. A duty the performance of which involved a regular and steady surplus of pain over pleasure on the whole, so that its non-observance would add to the general well-being, would cease to be a duty even for devil-worshippers. So, then, recognizing great variety in the sources of pleasure and in our estimates of their worthiness—matters which we need not further examine at present—we may fairly allow that all human action is primarily determined by a preference for pleasure before pain, a greater pleasure before a less, a less pain before a greater. This statement will, however, carry us but a very little way: it is barely the ABC of our subject. Its apparent simplicity is almost immediately complicated by other factors to which we must now turn.

So long as the pleasurable or painful objects or actions are actually present to consciousness it is literally true that the more pleasurable is preferred. At such times, too, an association is formed between the source of pleasure and the efforts needful for its continuance, so that the idea of the pleasurable object or occupation will afterwards revive the idea of the movements needful for its attainment or realization. But it may be that these movements are not immediately possible. A boy at school may, for example, think of the pleasures of the last holidays; but he cannot begin to realize them now, as, during the holidays themselves, he could go out fishing a second day prompted by the memory of his success the day before. In such a case, where the activity to which we are prompted is restrained, we are said to *desire*; unless distinctly conscious that we are helpless in the matter, and then we are more properly said to *wish*. Desire sets us at once to work devising ways and means, for desire is in itself a painful state of consciousness. You will note, however, that we have now passed into a new phase of things. When two or more desires conflict, our conduct is not primarily determined by the pleasure that will ensue in the future when the desires are satisfied, but by the pain that is present now and caused by the desires themselves. Nor can we say that *that* desire causes us most pain now, the object and end of which will afford us most pleasure when secured. For the frequent pursuit of an object constitutes the pursuit into a habit, so that the desire of the object may be strongest when the pleasure of its attainment has almost ceased; for desire is intensified by repetition, but pleasure very frequently diminishes, as novelty and freshness wear off. We have sufficiently melancholy instances of this in the reckless monomania of some collectors and the infatuation of "men of one idea," almost always an exaggerated idea, the realization of which will never justify a tithe of their efforts. So far is conduct determined by ideas from being proportional to the pleasure realized, that we may be driven by the impulse of desire to incur positive pain, as when curiosity leads us into the presence of horrors. Of this, Plato's story of Leontius in the *Republic* is an instance. The fascination of a precipice is probably only an extreme case of the same fact. The idea of an action tends to realize itself, the more imperatively the more vivid it is, whether pleasure or pain results. We have, then, in desire the uncontrolled working of our ideational mechanism: and the conduct to which it leads as little corresponds with what is pleasantest as its imagery corresponds with the external facts. All the causes of distortion and confusion at work in dreams are at work also in desire, and reason is as much needed to secure pleasure on the whole, or happiness, as it is to secure truth. Both in cognition and action there is a stage of falsehood and mistake, intermediate between the certainty of sense and the certainty of reason. When conduct is determined by present pleasure, the greater is preferred before the less; but when the actual pleasures or pains are absent and only represented by what survives of them in idea, and when these ideas are associated with impulses to action, the strength of which varies independently, then the less pleasure is often preferred before the greater. For our actions, in such cases, are determined by our ideas, and our ideas do not accurately correspond with realities. Moreover, a new set of pleasures and pains now enters: the pleasures and pains of desire and pursuit. As a rule, to follow the most urgent desire insures present pleasure or at least relief from the most pressing pain. But obedience to the fundamental law in this form may involve its frustration in the end; for desire entails continual self-denial and exertion in the present, followed perhaps by disappointment in the future. The creature that acts in obedience to present feeling and appetite may be said to secure all the well-being its resources admit of, but when obeying the extra-regarding impulses of desire it may cheat itself even of such well-being as this. To turn these extra-regarding impulses into a good they must be controlled, co-ordinated, and made to work to one end, and that not the attainment of these several objects but the happiness of self. In the language of Butler, who, along with Spinoza, has made the most important contributions to the psychology of conduct, they must be ruled by a cool self-love: or, in other words still, we must acquire the virtue of wisdom or prudence.

Let us now see what this rational principle of self-love is and how it is to be attained. A prudent man—and be it understood that we are concerned with nothing higher than prudence at present—is a man in whom the desire for the happiness of his own self is the strongest. Such a desire cannot exist at all till the conceptions of self and of happiness have been first formed. The child for some time has no such notions. It is not till it has made a considerable acquaintance with the world and with other persons, and is able to recollect all this experience in a connected fashion and distinctly recognize itself as the centre and thread of it all, that it can even begin to have a notion what self means. More reflexion and experience still are necessary before the child learns to care and to provide for self instead of following each individual impulse in its turn. It must often have felt the penalties of thoughtlessness and have clearly perceived that these might have been avoided or exchanged for some positive good by the exercise of forethought, before its natural impetuosity makes way for deliberation, and the claims of the future are allowed a voice in the present. And even this occurs but very partially at first. A burnt child dreads the fire, but it is none the safer from drowning because of that. In new cases, where the possible evils of haste cannot have been felt, there is no more prudence than before. Not till youth is well nigh past, and in many cases not even then, is the desire for happiness on the whole any effectual counterpoise to the impulses of the moment. The reason of all this is perfectly plain; impetuosity and rashness are not moral faults in youth, but the consequences of energy united with inexperience. In following their own desires, children do nothing wrong; we all do the same as far as we can. It is the business of the educator not to repress youthful energy but to make the young masters of themselves; not to root out their manifold desires but to subject them to reason. If the young could have the cautiousness of age, without its experience, they would have so much less experience when they became old themselves: the world would be played out or become Chinese. The child acts unless there are strong reasons for not acting, because activity is a delight; he takes everything for good till he finds the contrary. But for this spirit of hopeful, even playful, experiment we might all at this minute be so much *Globigerina* ooze at the bottom of the Atlantic; and if we were only sufficiently cautious I do not see how we should ever mend. The old, on the other hand, do not act unless there are strong reasons for activity, because activity is a trouble; they are apt to suspect everything is bad, till they find the contrary. Unless, therefore, they force themselves to know the child's nature, and avoid the tacit but false assumption that mind is the same thing in old and young, their first impulse will be to repress and restrain. Rousseau, who was aware of this disparity and longed for a treatise on the art of studying children, advised that a child's tutor should be young, because "there are not things enough in common between childhood and manhood[1]." Yet, if the young are not to be made wise by a general restraint laid upon their exuberant activity and spirit of adventure, neither are they to be made good by being deprived of the means and opportunities of following out their desires. To produce desolation and call it peace was once a ready way of subjugating a troublesome people; but we look for better things now. Apathy and listlessness, a puritanic indifference to all that is pleasurable in life, are no more prudence than monasteries are heaven. In making wisdom supreme we must leave it some

[1] R. H. Quick, *Essays on Educational Reformers*, p. 107.

subordinate impulses to be supreme over; and the more we leave, provided only they can be harmonized and controlled, the more perfect, because the more many-sided, will be the life.

But now let us study this so-called self-control, which is the major part of prudence, a little closer. First of all, I must object to the name; it is not self that we control but our extra-regarding impulses and desires which are opposed to the welfare of self. The power by which we control our desires is precisely the same as that by which we control our thoughts—the power, by means of attention, to determine the movements of our ideas. If we withdraw attention from the idea of an action we can refrain from the action, but when the idea passes a certain degree of intensity its actual movement ensues in spite of us. How little voluntary power of this kind children have at first we see in their inability to repress the manifestations of emotions. And, indeed, it is in this direction that the earliest lessons in voluntary control may be learnt, and especially in the repression of that most dismal business, crying. When a child cries simply because it is hurt or in pain, only good can result from training it to dry its tears, though this must be done not by severity, but by a quiet depreciation and indifference to the tears and noise. I need hardly say that crying, as a means of gaining its desires, should, as soon as possible, be treated as an offence. Merely intellectual occupation, again, is indirectly a source of moral strength, for, in learning to control our thoughts, we strengthen to some extent the power by which we can control our actions. Yet this alone would not carry us far, unless we had an *interest* in controlling them. Now, the educator can aid his pupil here in two ways: (*a*) by demanding obedience and (*b*) by drawing out for him and impressing the teaching of the pupil's own experience which he might else overlook.

The rising generation has to obey a good many rules, perhaps too many, for the benefit of its seniors; and this within due limits is neither unfair nor disadvantageous; the young learn in this way that others have rightful claims upon them. Apart from this, however, and even for their own sakes, it is a good thing to require obedience. To obey another will prepare them to obey reason, when the age of reason comes; but only if the obedience demanded is reasonable. This is a most important point. Children are our inferiors and are troublesome, and all the wiseacres in the world, since the beginning of time, have ordained that the young are for obedience, the old for command. In this respect, youth is very much in the position of an unenfranchised class; their own interests are very apt to suffer for want of due representation. The grave and reverend seniors who legislate for them would need to be more than human if—while intending only to stand *in loco rationis* and be eyes for the blind—they did not often insist on obedience, ostensibly for the good of the young people themselves, but which these have wit enough to see is more obviously, at all events, for some one else's good. If the question were asked me: Ought obedience to the mere will of another to be ever enforced? I should certainly incline to say 'No.' Where the mere will of another is concerned, sympathy and benevolence should be the determining motives; we should, in such a case, trust as much as possible to the child's personal affection and respect. For, otherwise, it seems to me, we are in danger of making him a slave. Kant's rule, I think, holds good here: Make no one a mere means to your own ends, but regard every one as an end in himself. When we command for the good of the community and the interests of right and order, there should be no appearance of personal inclination other than that of respect for the law. In this matter, young teachers are very liable to go astray; indeed, the natural love of command and power is so strong that it requires some watchfulness to avoid the enforcement of restrictions in themselves capricious and purposeless. At all events, the main advantage to the pupil of obedience is that he is not left to acquire by the slow and casual teaching of circumstances the habit of controlling his own impulsiveness; his opportunities for such exercise are enormously multiplied and are adapted to his condition and strength. As the dramatist condenses into a single play the incidents of a life-time, so the educator enables the pupil to rehearse his part in life during the early day of small things, and thus to avoid harder lessons and greater failures when the burden and heat of the day begin. But to secure this advantage, the obedience demanded should, as I have said, be *reasonable*; further the penalties of disobedience should, as clearly as possible, appear to be the natural and necessary consequences of disobedience, and not of the teacher's mere anger or resentment —except of course where he is directly injured or insulted, when due resentment is proper and salutary.

By reasonable commands, I do not mean only commands for which a reason is given, but commands which are as far as possible of the nature of general laws, and which justify themselves in the long run by the result. Legislation for special cases is always bad.

What we desire to quicken in the child is reverence for law, a deep sense of living under a reign of law, and a habit of prompt and cheerful law-observance. Restraint which does not promote this is worse than useless; and to say *A* must not do *X*, *B* must not do *Y*, *C* must not do *Z* to-day; and to-morrow to say *A* must not do *m*, *B* must not do *n*, *C* must not do *r*, will assuredly never promote either self-restraint or respect for law. Freedom is a good thing and we all desire it; the best blood that has ever been spilt has been shed for freedom, in some form or other. Restraint of freedom in one direction is only justifiable when it secures greater freedom on the whole. Now, a few strictly enforced, clearly-stated rules, that really are devised to secure the common weal, will not fail to commend themselves, in this respect, in the long run, though no exposition of their why and wherefore has been given. With very young children, it is impossible and undesirable to say why this or that is commanded or forbidden; for if one thing can be explained another cannot be, and authority must, therefore, in any case precede reason. Yet this makes it none the less desirable that the continual experience of authority should at length prove its reasonableness. It is in this way that Nature has trained the human race as a whole. If fire were to burn to-day and not to-morrow, if sometimes stones were good to eat and sometimes bread, if the sun went fizzing across the sky like a rocket one day and crawled back the opposite way like a snail the next, we should not now have much reason to boast of, not enough to make us wonder and protest at such vagaries. But the steady unbending uniformity of Nature, which ruthlessly punishes all who infringe her laws, and leads us on from strength rejoicing, *so long as we obey,—* this has made us wise at length and given us reason. And, if we look at all mankind, nay at all things living, we shall see that there is most reason where Nature's laws are best known; and more freedom and life, the more strictly they are obeyed. The educator, who has to supplement Nature's teaching, and direct his pupil's growth by the wisdom of the race, must follow Nature's plan. Within the bounds of rules, there should be ample liberty and security from uncertain and capricious interference; the rules should be fixed and clear; loyalty should increase, and disloyalty, inevitably and like fate, diminish the pupil's well-being. Of certain other aspects of authority I may have occasion to speak later on. All I have been concerned now to consider is how by demanding obedience from the young we may train them to be at length masters of themselves. And we may help them to this end in yet another way, namely, by drawing out and impressing the teaching of their own experience, which they might else overlook. In this, however, the utmost tact is required. We need to be clothed in humility and to have a very kindly heart if we are to do a man any good by pointing out his faults. With the young we are all very prone to air our superior wisdom at their expense and to wax mightily righteous as we expose and rebuke their folly. Perhaps the truth, however spoken, is wholesome in the end—wholesome physic; but it is the truth spoken in love that nurtures and strengthens. Yet, to speak the truth at all we must see things from the child's point of view. General disquisitions on morality are almost useless, while a lavish use of such epithets as 'stupid,' 'worthless,' 'wicked,' is simply brutal; such treatment wounds at first and hardens finally. Children are not only very sensitive, but they have also a strong feeling of pride, and it is extremely desirable that, so far as they can, they should keep it. It is this that makes gentle but not scathing satire such a useful way of bringing home to them a sense of their imprudence and lack of wisdom; it is in this way chiefly that they educate each other. A good-humoured stroke of wit is often more effectual and less depressing than a serious harangue. But, when seriousness is called for, it is of the utmost importance to take a generous view of the case, to assume, if possible, that the pupil's better self has been over-mastered, to recognize the difficulty as well as the necessity of self-rule; and, less as a lawgiver or a judge than as a friend, to suggest the way to succeed better next time. Nothing pleases a boy so much as, say, to learn from an experienced angler how to throw a fly; he admits the superior skill of his old Izaak Walton, and the latter, kindly soul, knows that it is hard and that the boy wants to learn. Now, we must picture out to ourselves some such relation as this, if we would understand one of the chief conditions of successful moral training. I really think that if the whole notion of culpability were to disappear and we came to regard the young as imperfect but not blameworthy—much as Robert Owen regarded every offender—the mischief that would ensue would hardly be greater than that now caused by our over-wrought notions of moral responsibility. Children are not responsible as you and I are, they are not wicked as you or I may be, they can acquire an interest in well-doing just as they can acquire an interest in knowledge, and will grow in wisdom as surely as they grow in stature, if only their minds are as wisely nurtured as their bodies. (Exceptions, no doubt, there are, in each case.) The conditions of interest are the same in the two cases. Tasks adapted to their present power of control, success, encouragement, help. Ideas, with which failure, pain and disheartening anxiety or fear are associated, will never be welcomed into consciousness, but will be kept out of mind as much as possible; and when these ideas enter they will depress and discourage, rather than brace for cheerful exertion. In directing the young, then, to gather moral lessons from their own experience we should, where we can, take these from their successes, rather than from their failures, and let hope and encouragement accompany even the severest rebukes; above everything, avoiding those vague and general references to desperate wickedness, bad ends and badness that has no ending, which only fill the young soul with an immoral terror and dread.

LECTURE X

VOLITION, SENSE OF JUSTICE, AND BENEVOLENCE

In the last lecture we saw that the earliest and most fundamental law of all human action—sometimes inaccurately termed the law of self-preservation—is to seek pleasure and avoid pain. So far as the life of sense extends this law holds simply and absolutely. But when, as with human beings is soon the case, we rise to actions determined not by present sensations but by ideas, to actions directed to future ends, the law admits of a twofold reference, and becomes in fact ambiguous. If we say that our desires are directed towards pleasure, it is false; desires are directed to the attainment of definite objects and the pleasure that will ensue after the object is attained is at most but one factor in the desire and often not the chief. If we say that the more pressing or painful desire determines our action, this is true; but the satisfaction of such desire may be a source of further pain rather than pleasure. Thus, obedience to the law of self-preservation on the higher level of idea-prompted action often entails the actual frustration of the law in after experience; desire alone is a far worse caterer than sense. The man who is the slave of desire probably endures ten-fold the wretchedness and disappointment of the brute that is in all things obedient to present sensation. Yet the source of the mischief is also the source of the cure; and not merely so, it is the source also of greater and more permanent good. For, as our ideas grow, besides desires for this or that object or pursuit, we attain to the desire of well-being on the whole, and the more this central desire gains in strength the more are we set upon controlling and ruling those extra-regarding desires which are directed to the attainment of some external object and end. So that even the man who cares for nothing but sensual gratification will yet, if he is reasonable enough to think of his general welfare, restrain the appetite of to-day in the interests of to-morrow. Such is the man whom we stigmatize as an Epicurean and a hedonist, the man who by calculation and foresight, looking before and after, seeks to secure for himself upon the whole a maximum of pleasure, a minimum of pain, and who to do this curtails the enjoyment of the moment or voluntarily submits to present pain. Although of course a very unworthy life, yet we must not overlook the fact that it is in one sense a reasonable life, and the man who should steadily live on such principle would assuredly be a man of character, that is to say, his actions would be consistent and we should be able to foretell them.

Now, it is quite worth while to notice this type of character, because though neither elevated nor common, it presents us with what we may call practical reason in its simplest form. As the *Amphioxus* is the lowliest vertebrate, so the Epicurean affords the lowliest example of rational conduct: he is a moral *Amphioxus*. There is only one thing in which this creature, the *Amphioxus*, or lancelet, can boast itself superior to the molluscs; it has no brain, *but it has the beginnings of a backbone.* So with the hedonist; there is nothing worthy in his life except definiteness and self-control, otherwise he is no better than the brute. But, just on this account, he shews us more clearly wherein the essence or form of character consists—namely, in self-rule, rule by self, autonomy. To train to good habits in this direction and in that without training to self-rule is to produce a moral automaton, not a man. It is a mistake precisely analogous to that of teaching facts instead of teaching to think; though easier both for the teacher and the taught, it is incomparably less valuable. Hence it was that I began by laying stress upon this element in moral training. Self-control is the very root and backbone of character; moreover, though it is a sad thing when character never gets beyond that lowest stage in which pleasure *in the narrower sense* is the aim, yet it is with this stage that it has to begin. Children have to take many of their earliest lessons in morals in controlling their desires for pleasures to-day in the interests of pleasure to-morrow, or pleasure on the whole. Yet the sooner they get beyond this level of things the better; the educator's problem as regards animal appetites is not merely to give power to control them, but to make them easily controllable by preventing them from assuming the place of permanent interests. Pestalozzi's advice in this respect is psychologically sound. The child's hunger and thirst are to be relieved before they become urgent, so that its mind shall never be long occupied by the claims of its lower life. For if these be not satisfied till they have grown clamorous, they must necessarily engage a disproportionate share of the child's active interest in their behalf. However, there are few homes or schools so badly regulated as to make emphasis on this point necessary; and yet, in another way, it is deliberately set aside and, it seems to me, erroneously. Locke, for example, recommends that children should be fed on the plainest food, such as water gruel or a piece of brown bread, often without butter, for breakfast, and thinks that in this way they will come to prefer such food. Doubtless, if he could have gone to a school-treat, he would have changed his mind. It is singular that Locke, although both a medical man and a psychologist, is yet when discussing the physical training of children, oftener wrong than right. Herbert Spencer is here far superior to Locke: variety in food is good, as he says, not only for children but for everybody, and the fondness children manifest for sweets and fruit rests ultimately on a physiological need. Even if this were not so, I should, however, still urge that these desires should be gratified before they become excessive, so that they may never come to engross much of the child's thought and care. It is on this account that elaborate discussions about dress and dinners, in the presence of the young at all events, are best avoided. Not that dress and dinners are small matters in themselves by any means; they furnish the moralist and the artist with a great field; but they are so liable, where they are matters of definite concern too early, to be made inordinately important. All the same, the happy mean, the due balance between too much and too little regard for these things, is not to be reached by positive repression and enforced asceticism; for pent-up desires are always dangerous, and to empty the mind of evil will not ensure its being filled with good. Let the lower pleasures have all along their natural place, and the brightness and cheerfulness they will bring will be sources of strength and make self-control easier. To prevent them having more than their due place higher interests must be quickened alongside of them. And this remark brings us back to the course of moral development which we were before observing.

The perfect Epicurean is a very rare animal, just as his analogue the lancelet is a very rare fish, rare in the sense of being reduced to a single species. The man who has character enough to seek the pleasure of sense wisely has usually too much brains to seek such pleasures alone. For, as I have said, with the growth of ideas come new pleasures and pains, and these steadily and continually in all but the worst of mankind gain the ascendant over the lower interests of sense. Now, I hardly know any point upon which there has been more confusion among moralists than upon this— a confusion due largely to a neglect of psychology, but partly to the ambiguity of the word 'pleasure.' But let us look first at a parallel confusion where the relations are plainer. We should agree that, whatever life means, there is more life in two oysters than in one of them, or in two crabs than in either one. Yet, before we could say how many oysters it would take to give us as much life as there is in one crab, we should have to decide what we mean by life. Let us, for mere illustration's sake, suppose that in some fool's paradise or other we had a small planetoid committed to our charge and had to see that it exhibited as much life as possible, how should we decide between oysters and crabs? Biologists tell us that the most complex organism consists ultimately of proto- plasm, which is the physical basis of life. Should we, then, go in for a maximum of protoplasm? Clearly not, for this would be to make organization indifferent, and that it is not indifferent these same biologists tell us; for protoplasm, they say, as far as it can and as fast as it can, begins to organize itself. There ensues a division of functions such as occurs when a shipload of emigrants settle on an island; one becomes fisherman, another shepherd, a third builder and so on. We must suppose, similarly, a lump of protoplasm is better off in which one part is differentiated into nerve, another into muscle and so on. In a word, we have to recognize not only quantity of life—which we might measure by the quantity of oxygen consumed—but quality of life, for which no material measure exists. We should call that the higher life which pertained to the more complex structure and in which the higher functions—sensibility and movement—were most ad- vanced. Now, *mutatis mutandis*, the same thing holds of what we call pleasures. If by pleasures we mean desirable or preferable objects, then these unquestionably differ qualitatively; if by pleasure we mean the mere intensity of feeling apart from the objects or occasions of it, then, no doubt, this is simply quantitative. The mere thrill of delight consequent on discovering a new fact in science may be no greater than that of coming unexpectedly on a bank of strawberries, but it does not, therefore, follow that one would not be very definitely preferred before the other. The fact is that though we are all along preferring a more pleasurable state of conscious- ness before a less, the content of our consciousness is continually changing, not to say widening and deepening; the delights of childhood cease to please in manhood, because the occupations of manhood are higher, albeit the pleasurable feeling may be no greater. This fact, too, may be illustrated from life. In advancing from a less perfect to a more perfect organization, the tendency at any one moment is simply towards more life, simply self-preservation; but the life attained continuously and imperceptibly modifies the self that is to be preserved. The creature thinks only of filling its stomach; Nature sees to it that, in so doing, it advances the perfection of its structure. So, too, we may say that man, even when he steadily and consciously seeks his own happiness, is yet thereby led by that power that shapes our ends to secure his own perfection. This is true of man as a whole when we compare the history of the race century by century. Nevertheless, it is far, indeed, from being true of the individual, who in the direct pursuit of happiness solely may ruin or degrade himself, and only aid the perfection of others by serving as a beacon or a warning. For Nature, though reasonable in her ends, appears to us to work blindly and slowly in her use of means; at all events, when we have rightly interpreted her aim we can by the light of reason attain the end more quickly and with less apparent sacrifice. It is the prerogative of reason thus to help or hinder.

But what, you will be asking, is the drift of all this? The outcome of it all is that to seek your own perfection is wiser, more prudent, more reasonable than to seek your own happiness, even though common sense should declare happiness preferable, supposing the two could clash. Yet, let us not be in too great a hurry. The point from which we started was the continuous development of newer and intellectually more complex interests as our stock of ideas enlarges. In consequence of this, we cannot quantitatively compare pleasurable states in different stages of life, nor even in different frames of mind, so as to know which is preferable: for the preference depends on the two stages or frames of self and these differ in kind rather than in degree. The mere intensity of the gratifications (even if we could know that apart) would be no guide at all. Thus, in the only sense in which pleasures are commensurable—a sense in which, strictly speaking, we ought not to talk of pleasures, but only of the feeling of pleasure—the intensity of pleasure is no general guide to happiness; it is at best a guide from moment to moment, while we are engaged with interests of the same class. It may help me to decide between Scarborough and Brighton, or between cherry-tart or pine-apple cream; but it will not help me to decide for my well-being on the whole. To this end, I must take counsel with reason and knowledge, which will aid me for the whole course of life, as the compass aids the mariner; they only will enable me to go straight towards my end, instead of everlastingly following all the ins and outs of the coast, never able to lose sight of the pleasure produced.

Those who have seen what service reason renders have often overlooked the fundamental principle of self-preservation—that unless happiness is secured, reason is not justified. Those who have seen the fundamental principle of self-preservation have often lacked the faith to discern that reason alone can guide us towards the end. But, though theoretical moralists have confused the two, the confusion is not common in actual life; for, as I said just now, the consistent Epicurean is altogether rare. The man who has reason enough to plan for his happiness as a whole soon finds his reason direct him to the development of his own nature as the means. And this implies an apparent departure from the end itself, like casting your bread upon the waters only to find it after many days. There is, then, no sort of pious fraud in diverting the young from concern for their own happiness and interesting them rather in the unfolding of their own powers and in the great questions of the age in which they live. There is much truth in the paradox of the great teacher, when rightly interpreted, "whosoever will save his life shall lose it, but whosoever will lose his life for my sake, the same shall save it."

But we may look at the course of moral development from another point of view, and one which will lead us round naturally to matters of immediate educational interest. If we consider mankind generally or the best races of mankind, and especially the best men among these races, the men who are themselves the happiest and whose lot we covet, we shall find that such men are men whose hands are full of work. And so far is this from being a necessity, the less of the two evils, so far is work from being a curse, that we find idleness and unhappiness are usually combined, even where external goods are no ways lacking. On the other hand, those who work tell us that they find their pleasure in it. The secret of happiness, then, it would seem lies not in looking after happiness but in occupation. At first, no doubt, our pleasures are chiefly, though by no means solely, of the receptive kind and much of our childish activity is directed towards these delights of sense. Yet, by degrees, the pleasures of activity become more engrossing; and gradually, too, as the power to think and reason extends, the activity in which we find our interest is activity in which thought is concerned, whether it pass beyond thinking or not. At first, we seek things, the pleasures of sense, because they are good; later on, things become good because we seek them, because, as rational beings, they have an interest for us. Nobody has put this better or seen it more clearly than did Aristotle over two thousand years ago: let me quote a summary of his view as given by Grote: "The man who is in the active exercise of virtue derives his pleasure from the performance of that which is the appropriate business of humanity, so that all his pleasures are *conformable to the pleasures natural to man* and, therefore, consistent with each other: whereas the pleasures of most people are contradictory and inconsistent with each other, because they are not conformable to our nature[1]."

If, then, we say that the first point in moral training is to make the young masters of themselves, to secure to them that internal freedom which is only possible when all the desires and impulses are under control, the second point assuredly must be to lead them to consecrate themselves to work, work that can engage and retain the interests of a rational being. By the first they will attain character, by the second worth, that is, become entitled to the respect of themselves and their fellow-men. Yet, as I have so often said, this cannot be done by preaching to them about the dignity of work. Encouragement of this kind is, indeed, not to be neglected; history and biography will furnish stirring examples enough to shew that work is not only the law of our being but its health and glory. But, before and beyond all this, the young must be trained to work themselves, and not only this, but they must be so trained that they will *like* work. "These be brave words," you will say, perhaps ironically, but none the less I hold them to be sober truth. However hard to attain, nothing short of this is what the educator must aim at; and none need take it more to heart than those who have the responsibility of educating the wealthy youth of England. To like work you must have work that you like, and the school-teacher's first concern should be to have every scholar interested in something, in which, therefore, he can safely demand continued exertion. Indeed, this is a duty for parents before the school-teacher comes on the scene at all. We must not, however, confuse work with play; when tired of one game, there is no objection to taking up another, but desultoriness in work is to be strenuously discouraged: nay, work that is desultory ceases to be work. This, however, only makes it the more

[1] G. Grote, *Aristotle*, edited by A. Bain and G. Croom Robertson, 3rd ed., p. 504.

important that the work should be interesting, for it is impossible permanently to override the fundamental law that voluntary activity must be pleasurable. It is desirable, no doubt, that the work with which the pupil occupies himself should be that which will best fit him for higher work hereafter; better, say, that an ordinary boy should give his strength to literature than to drawing; nor will it, in the great number of cases, be difficult to secure an interest in the graver studies, if they are wisely taught by a sympathetic and earnest teacher. We know sufficient of human nature by this time to feel pretty sure that if the greater part of a class is not attracted to literature, science or history, it is because these subjects are badly taught. And, at all events, if a child is left to grow up without the habit of work it must inevitably sink both intellectually and morally; and not only so, it must drag down others too[1].

Strength of will and energetic love of work are, of course, not all that moral training has to secure, even when we consider only the self-regarding virtues. But it would be superfluous to discuss, for example, what constitutes an occupation worthy or unworthy. To do this would be to undertake an outline of practical morality. These two points, however, do seem to me to need insisting upon, because, while they are the life and marrow of all robust character, they are liable to be lost sight of in a natural anxiety to 'inculcate' definite virtues. Indeed, since decision and energy of character have been possessed only too often by men remarkable for anything but virtue, and as they are, moreover, often very troublesome traits in a scholar, I am not sure that school-teachers are not sometimes weak enough to discourage them; quiet, docile children are so much easier to manage.

But the psychological process by which character consolidates, is by the formation of habits; and, though I have referred to this process a good deal incidentally, it will be well, at least for a moment, to consider it more directly. Still, it need hardly be for more than a moment, for, if we understand the general law of the association of ideas, there is nothing substantially new in the formation of habits. In acquiring a new manual dexterity, for example, all that we do is to repeat, in a certain order, a number of simple movements till the complex constituted by the whole of them is firmly and securely fixed, so that it can be attended to at once, much as a complex of ideas, which have been united in a concept, is attended

[1] Cf. Thring, *Education and School*, 2nd ed., p. 113.

to. When this stage of proficiency is reached, the habit is completely formed; the action is then said to be automatic or mechanical, and attention to its constituent movements is no longer necessary, indeed, hardly possible. As at first attention and effort were necessary to bring about the association, so now only by attention and effort can the association be dissolved and the habit unlearnt. And what is true in such an extreme case as that of acquiring feats of skill is really true of life as a whole. We tend to become more and more creatures of habit, with fixed interests and tastes and ways of work. This, which is certainly not an unmixed evil, is also far from being an unmixed good.

Now, I am not going to remark upon the importance of training to good habits and of checking the acquisition of bad ones, because all important as this is, everybody is awake to it or at least aware of it; and, if you were not disposed to act up to your knowledge, it would not be my province to exhort you to do so. What I rather want to urge is that even training to good habits is anything but an unmixed advantage. I did casually raise this point just now in passing, but it is worth returning to. There is just the same anxiety abroad to save the young from the risks of acting for themselves as there is to save them from the risks of finding truth for themselves, which is indeed a form of acting. As correct opinions are duly instilled into them, so too are they habituated to correct conduct. All I say is that if the young gain by this they lose also, which amounts to no more than saying that there is a right and a wrong way even of training to virtue. On this, as on so many other points overlooked by the traditional theory, Rousseau was wiser than his generation, and this only makes one the more angry with him for his extravagance. "Emile," he says, "acts from his own thoughts and not from the dictation of others." And again, "if your head always directs your pupil's hands, his own head will become useless to him." But no sane person, I presume, would now propose to leave the young to act from their own thoughts, as Rousseau, with his absurd doctrine of the supremacy of nature over reason, does. No, all that we need to be concerned about is that habits should not smother spontaneity and reason too. What are called 'goody children' and the disastrous wrecks of many such, instances of which most of us, I suppose, can readily recall, shew us what is the evil to avoid. Perhaps, it might be described in a word as the evil of substituting habits for principles. For the particular cases habits are surer in action, but for new cases they are powerless. At first, habit must precede reason, for habits can be formed before reason is possible, but as the age of reason begins, habits must follow reason. With very young children, as I said in my last lecture, it is undesirable to give reasons; authority is for them the best of reasons. Yet care is needed that this deference to mere authority be not continued too long. We all know the story of the silly crow who would not let her young try to fly till she was sure that they would not tumble out of the nest. It is not, however, altogether on this account that reason is not appealed to; the cause, I fear, often is that it is more troublesome and involves beside a certain surrender of authority, to say nothing of inviting reprisals when the teacher forgets himself.

Yet there is a further evil still in over much zeal to cultivate good habits in the young, and that is the danger which we most of us begin to dread as we get older—shall I call it *fossilization?* But the danger and the cure are, in this case, also, in the main the same as in the last. We want to avoid imprisoning the soul in a set machinery of habit as the genius in the Arabian Nights was sealed up in a bottle; we want to have our habits behind us fixing our work, not before us barring our advance. The analogy of the body is not uninstructive here. Nature starts us with such instinctive dexterities as shall enable us to acquire more, and it is our fault if we let this spontaneity languish for want of exercise. As a rule, the acquisition of one bodily dexterity rather helps than hinders the acquisition of another. So it must be with the mind; old interests must beget new ones, that is, our interests must have in them a life-long power of growth and development. At this point we see again how close is the connexion between intellectual and moral training. The wider a man's circle of ideas, the longer he will be fresh, and still in every sense alive, growing and not mentally stagnant, borne along by newly acquired energy and not merely by the momentum of the past, with which, perhaps, he gradually parts in obstructing the advance of others. But by wide circles of ideas I do not mean such a farrago of fact and fancy as he compounds who merely reads everlastingly, but ideas which furnish material for thought and action; for without these we may get mentally dense and ponderous, but we grow no more.

So far we have considered moral training without taking account of the pupil's relation to others. What morality requires of him, in this respect, might, perhaps, be summed up in the words, justice and benevolence. I am not going to trouble you with a disquisition on justice. However much you might be puzzled if you found yourself cross-questioned on the subject by some modern Socrates, I do not doubt, or at all events must be content to suppose, that you know what justice is well enough for our present purpose. All I wish to do, and that very briefly, is to urge the cultivation of what has been called a 'passion for justice' even from the first. It is the opportunity for such cultivation as the playground affords that constitutes one of its chief educational merits, and that is a very bad school indeed in which fair play is not supreme; for as love of truth is the root of all intellectual virtue, so is love of justice the foundation of the social virtues, and so far more important than benevolence that benevolence is not safe without it. Yet benevolence is easier to teach and can be taught earlier, for justice is intellectually a somewhat complex idea, whereas bene-volence implies only good nature[1]. Hence, as Locke acutely suggests, we can only suppress the natural injustice of little children by encouraging them to be generous and liberal. In fact, the pro-cedure throughout must be here largely negative, so far as justice alone is concerned; this virtue itself is, indeed, largely negative: children learn to love justice by learning to hate injustice. But it is indispensable to this end that they should be themselves justly dealt with by their parents and teachers; if all the injustice they have to hate is the injustice they suffer, they will infallibly recoup themselves by being tyrants and usurpers and partial in their turn. To treat them fairly, check their own unfairness, and encourage to a generous unselfishness, is all that can be done for some time. Yet, when youth begins, the sacredness of justice should be taught, and justice be everywhere given and demanded till an earnest zeal for it be evoked, which could appropriate the words, *fiat justitia ruat coelum*. And there need be no fear that the feeling will be too strong, for, as Mill has truly said, the most indispensable of all necessaries after physical nutrition is security; and security is not secure without a passion for justice. It is from the sentiment of justice more than from anything else that we derive the conception

---

[1] "It has always appeared to me that the love of justice is one of the rarest of all good qualities, I mean the love of it with full and commanding strength. I should almost dare to say that there are five generous men for one just man. The beauty of justice is the beauty of simple form: the beauty of generosity is heightened with colour and every accessory, but they always tend to divert from justice. The man who strongly loves justice must love it for its own sake, and such a love makes of itself a character of simple grandeur to which it is hard to find an equal." From a letter of W. E. Gladstone, written on the occasion of the death of Lord Aberdeen.

of 'ought' which is the cardinal notion of all morality; and it is not too much to say that it is impossible to train to fidelity to duty at all while the love of justice is absent. It is highly important, too, to observe that even though justice is only justified by its activity—so much so that in special cases where our common-sense notions of justice fail to guide us, in casuistry in short, we all resort to considerations of utility for a solution—yet no theory of utilitarianism can dispense with the *sentiment* of justice. It is this, the spirit and love of fairness, that has to be cultivated, the ability to estimate the balance of advantages is a very much smaller matter. We might as well propose to substitute science for the guidance of our taste in the matter of food. If a man asks me to try a new kind of toadstool I ask him to have it analysed first, but I make no such request in presence of a dish of mushrooms. It shews an utter misappreciation not only of utilitarianism but of science altogether to suppose that the truth of the utilitarian theory would diminish the value of the sentiment of justice in the least.

LECTURE XI

DISCIPLINE AND AUTHORITY

Unus homo, nullus homo, said a Cambridge philosopher over two hundred years ago; a human being by himself would soon cease to be a human being at all. To train to perfect humanity we must evoke an interest in human kind; even in common speech, selfishness and humanity are opposed. And rightly so, for the normal man is not wholly selfish; on the contrary, even without training, he is often actuated by genuinely disinterested and unselfish motives. He does things, that is to say, which he would not do, which he would not account it reasonable to do, if he were concerned only for his own happiness. The spring of such unselfish action is sympathy, or fellow-feeling; and, as feeling is either pleasurable or painful, so sympathy may be either rejoicing with them that do rejoice or weeping with them that weep. Sympathy, it hardly needs to be said, implies a previous experience of the joys or sorrows which we feel again in imagination when they are actually experienced by others; it implies, too, the ability to infer these feelings from the manifestation of them, it may be in tears or smiles, in laughter or in groans, in choked utterance or in shouts of joy. But, besides previous experience and the ability to imagine another's experience by recalling our own, sympathy involves a further and more complicated act of imagination still. We must identify *ourselves* in imagination with those with whom we sympathize. Even when we perfectly realize the circumstances there is no sympathy without this, but simply understanding. The less we have in common with another, the less readily or completely can we sympathize with him, however familiar we may be with the causes of his joy or sorrow. A wide range of sympathy is, therefore, not possible in young children, though, so far as their experience and imagination carry them, their sympathy at least with others' sufferings is ready and deep. I doubt if it is desirable or necessary specially to cultivate this aspect of sympathy by harrowing stories that melt the young soul to pity. It is true, though puzzling, that sympathy with suffering affords a subtle pleasure—what Herbert Spencer has called 'the luxury of pity,' a pleasure in which it is dangerous to indulge too freely. When the suffering attains to tragic sublimity the harm is less, nay such fiction has on young and old alike, as Aristotle tells us, a purifying effect. Yet affecting tales become mischievous if they give a romantic tinge to common misery, which, at all events, a child may fail to discern in the wretchedness it may see in its walks abroad. The most callous people in the world, I believe, are those who weep over any new novel. As a general rule, it is dangerous to one's moral integrity to express, under the influence of strong feeling, more than we are likely in cooler moments to perform; and we ought, on the one hand, to expect the young to carry out their generous resolutions and, on the other, to warn them beforehand of the difficulties. It must, then, surely be injurious habitually to awaken strong emotions which should naturally lead to action, when, from the nature of the case, action is impossible; even if such fictitious cases did nothing to blunt the feeling for real ones.

But, while children are naturally ready enough to sympathize with such suffering as they can understand, they are by no means so ready to enter into any joy of another which they do not directly share. And this one-sidedness unfortunately is far from disappearing with short frocks and jackets; for, as Jean Paul puts it: *Zum Mitleid genügt der Mensch, zur Mitfreude gehört ein Engel* (man is equal to sharing another's sorrow, it requires an angel to rejoice in another's joy). Envy awakes to check sympathy with another's good fortune, but there is no such certain obstacle to sympathy with trouble from which we are free. Now, envy has to be conquered; yet in itself, for all that, it is not immoral, but the natural and necessary outcome of our mental constitution, as a little reflexion will shew. The sight of a good we do not ourselves possess is apt at any time to awaken longing desires and so to cause us pain and discontent; but when, at the same time, we can in imagination identify ourselves with the person whose happier circumstances has quickened our desire, the unreasonable idea arises that what we so easily imagine might really have been but for his intervention. And this is the essence of envy, the frequent parent of hate. Hence, we are especially prone to envy those with whom we can most readily identify ourselves, namely, our own friends; and, again, envy arises more easily the more the coveted good appears to have been bestowed by chance or fortune, and the less it has been clearly earned by merit—one among the many psychological facts which make gambling such a diabolical pursuit. Envy, then, being thus natural, we must not be surprised that children manifest it, and are apt to manifest it strongly.

Besides very carefully avoiding all favouritism—the influence of which is most pernicious upon the morality of the young—we must seek to counteract envy by encouraging sympathy with others' happiness, a more valuable and a more difficult piece of training than the training to sympathy with pain and misery. For, if you will put up with a little more psychology, you will see that precisely that aspect of self-love which makes the one form of sympathy more difficult makes the other easier. To see another the victim of a misfortune which was within an ace of falling to our own lot naturally awakens not only self-gratulation but a regard for the sufferer, as if he had been our scape-goat. It is easy to feel kindly towards another who thus indirectly increases our own self-complacency; but we have to forget ourselves if we are to retain kindly feelings towards one whose more brilliant success or good fortune throws our own into the shade, and reduces it to comparative misfortune or failure. If his success leads us to think of ourselves, we shall envy him; only while we think primarily of him and his gratification can we rejoice with him.

On the means by which the habit of entering into the lives of others is to be developed I can only make two or three disconnected remarks. First of all, it is desirable as little as possible to direct the child's attention specially to itself. As we have already seen, its own welfare lies largely in occupations which entail self-forgetfulness; idle people are not only the most miserable but also the most selfish. Selfishness is a habit, which may be encouraged or discouraged, like any other. If the child's circumstances are such that it is obliged to look well after itself or suffer in consequence, or if it finds itself an object of conversation and is used to be waited upon hand and foot by parents and servants, then self will naturally have a large place and the first place in its thoughts; in the one case from necessity, in the other by imitation and unconscious inference. Still, it must be allowed that those who have to struggle in order to live can sympathize with others in difficulty all the better, for they know from personal experience what hardship is. I question if the gutter boy who lives in St Giles's is not often more kindly to his companions than his richer brother in St James's. The most favourable atmosphere for unselfishness is that in which there are most opportunities for acts of kindness and most pleasures and interests that can be shared and be heightened by being shared. Happy is the home or school pervaded by such an atmosphere; where each is led to care first for the rest, and where there are many pursuits in which all can join. The surest way to sympathize with another's welfare is to promote it; and the children in a home and the pupils in a school should be encouraged actively to promote each other's happiness. But there should be no rewards for such good conduct; indeed, that is apt to be a very spurious form of virtue which is only coaxed into activity by external rewards and good conduct prizes. Justice is entitled to no reward, for it is but yielding others their due; and generosity becomes a semblance and a sham when the self-denial it entails is compensated by anything more than the pure pleasure of benevolence. Its reality consists in its spontaneousness; and, as it cannot be demanded by pains or penalties, neither should it be by the indirect penalty of rewards foregone. For the young, at all events, it is more important to encourage the habit of positively ministering to happiness than that of simply neutralizing unhappiness. As it is harder to sympathize with joy than with sorrow, so there is something more creatively beneficent, as it were, in increasing happiness than in diminishing unhappiness. And the greater carries the less, but not the less the greater. The man who will put his hand deep into his pocket to give the children of the poor a romp in the fields is more likely to care for a starving and plague-stricken population than one who is indifferent to such juvenile merry-making. Relieving distress is decidedly the more selfish as it is the more common form of beneficence. The best preparations for a manhood possessed by the enthusiasm of humanity are (*a*) a happy childhood and (*b*) a childhood the happiness of which largely consists in making others already happy happier still[1].

So far we have left the personality of the teacher in the background, and have regarded him mainly as an impersonal influence, theoretically perfect, directing the intellectual and moral growth of his scholars. But the facts are, of course, far otherwise, and we must look at things as they are. "As is the teacher, so is the scholar," it has been said: no other educational instrument is so powerful as the teacher's personal influence; and, where this is faulty, it matters not what else is free from blame. I do not propose now to speak of the teacher's power to make his special subject attractive by the liveliness of his own presentation of it, but simply of the power of his example in moulding the character of his pupils. Imitativeness is at all times an important factor in determining

[1] Cp. I. Taylor, *Home Education*, 5th ed., p. 37, *fin.*

human conduct and tastes, and is always strongest where judgment is weakest. Children and savages are the best mimics, and acquire much by imitation that they lack the intelligence to comprehend. "We are all," says Locke, "a sort of camelions, that still take a tincture from things near us: nor is it to be wondered at in children who better understand what they see than what they hear." This last remark of Locke's reminds us that that superior impressiveness of facts over words, which we had to insist upon in intellectual training, makes the teacher's conduct also more impressive than his precepts. Even while the teacher is aiming to make his pupils self-governing beings, he cannot avoid exerting an unconscious influence upon their lives. And, after all, the man who does most to shape his own character often does less towards it than his parents, teachers and friends have done. His character determines his choice of friends and friends react on his character. I must say, once more, that it does not fall to my province to exhort teachers so to live that even their very presence shall be a power for good. All I am concerned to do is to call attention to this influence which the teacher's position gives him, whether he will or no; and, unhappily, there is but a very narrow neutral margin— if there is any—between influence for good and influence for bad in this region of things. Nitrogen is a perfectly harmless substance; but, for all that, it suffocates life as effectually and almost as soon as other gases that are rank poison. Many of us, I fear, have done a great deal of harm in this way, ignorantly and unintentionally. And, unless a school-teacher is at the pains to reflect upon the effect of his daily intercourse with his scholars and to understand how things look from the scholars' point of view, he is almost sure to settle down into a perfunctory routine, in which the individuality of his pupils and all that lies beyond the class-work count for nothing. Mr Quick speaks more than once of the narrowing influence of the teacher's occupation. "Hence it appears," he says in one place, "that a man who set out with the notion of developing all the power of his pupils' minds, thinks in the end of nothing but getting them to work out equations and to do Latin exercises without false concords." One of the cures for this, no doubt, is, as Mr Quick suggests, to relieve teachers from overwork, so that they may have a chance of preserving their geniality and good spirits to the end. Perhaps, indeed, till this is done it may be hopeless to look for any great improvement; and yet I suspect the too common misconception of the school-teacher's first duty is largely to blame for the perfunctory mode in which he sometimes works. For let me say once more that the aim of the school is not mere instruction, nor even intellectual training alone, but the complete unfolding of the pupil's human nature, till the time arrives when he ought to assume full command of himself. To understand, then, the part which the educator's personality must play in this work let us endeavour to represent to ourselves how the teacher appears to the taught. If any man needs to exclaim with Burns,

> "*Oh wad some power the giftie gie us*
> *To see oursels as ithers see us,*"

it is the school-teacher when those others are his pupils: for surely one of the first steps towards understanding the young is to know how they regard us. The natural attitude of the young towards their elders is one of respect and dependence, and the natural experience of childhood tends to deepen these feelings. To his elders the child has looked at every turn for support, information and advice; and the height of his ambition is to be himself every inch a man. Nothing affords him more pleasure than the friendship of grown-up people, those of them at least who understand how to be friends with children. Now, it may be that the boy has had the misfortune to be led to regard the school-teacher as his natural enemy; but of this he is soon disillusionized, if the school-teacher does not prove an enemy in fact; and the goodwill the pupil shews to others will be not long withheld from his teacher. None reciprocate kindness sooner than the young, and none are more acutely susceptible to the sunshine or gloom of countenance and manner. A teacher, then, who is naturally genial and unaffected starts with everything in his favour, and the danger rather is that he will jeopardize his authority in his anxiety to begin on good terms with his pupils rather than that he will repel them by the earnestness of his manner—especially if he understands his subject and knows how to teach it. If he can make his class like their work and want to advance in it—and half the battle here is to proportion the work to their strength and keep them actively and successfully occupied— he will by this alone attach them to him. But, instead of this, teachers sometimes assume that work *must* be a bore, and act as if the problem were to secure their pupil's goodwill in spite of classwork and by an extra agreeable and kindly manner out of school. Such a feeble faith and paltry proceeding must often fail and never deserves to succeed. Such a man, whether he knows it or not, is really a perverter of youth.

For the really honest and able teacher, the great difficulty is the maintenance of discipline. And here, of course, I do not pretend that there is any substitute for experience. None the less, there are sundry theoretical considerations that may enable him to buy his experience on cheaper terms and turn it to better account. One thing in particular is often forgotten, namely, that, when dealing with a single offender, the teacher's conduct is judged by the public opinion of a whole class or a whole school. It is this public opinion which makes everything the teacher does so important and it is with this that he always has to reckon in the end. I do not pretend myself to understand it, or even to estimate roughly the elements of which it is composed. It is less enlightened, more prejudiced, more liable to be swayed by passion or individual influence, than even the public opinion of the larger world outside school. Noble sentiments turned inside out and in very ignoble guises have often a place in it; the infatuation of trade-unionists or communists has its counterpart here, and the lawlessness and cunning of the savage are not wanting. Obedience is apt to be judged contemptible, and indolence and contumacy to be admired as spirited and manly; freedom is confounded with licence, leniency with weakness, truthfulness with treachery. By this tribunal the teacher is often judged, without the possibility of defence, or even the suspicion that the *ex parte* statements of a disconcerted idler are not evidence. A teacher who deals with every case fairly upon its merits, and ignores this public opinion, only half does his work and may lay up trouble for himself in days to come. He who allows himself to be stung by its injustice and prejudice into resentment and coercion is guilty of a species of civil war and may not improbably be ruined. There is nothing for it but an almost divine patience, the most unswerving justice, and the absence of everything that can be construed into a signal for revolt.

But, of course, the real problem is to create and guide this public opinion of the school oneself. And in this work of the schoolmaster there are many interesting analogies with the work of the statesman. The schoolmaster is, in fact, a statesman in miniature, the only statesman who takes office without studying statecraft or the nature of those whom he has to govern. Herbert Spencer somewhere remarks that the style of school-discipline in any age or country is always approximately parallel with that of the national government. This may be a hasty generalization; at all events, in these days, when schoolboys read newspapers and discuss politics, it may be such an approximation is both possible and desirable. Yet, without entering upon any question so wide as this, we may be satisfied that no school government is good that is not strong, the laws of which are not clear and defined, and the penalties "certain, speedy and sharp." The schoolmaster is at an immense advantage who has such an abstract power at his back, and his advantage is greater still if the rules of the school give him the opportunity of practically evincing respect for law by his own conformity. In such a position, he may do much to shape the common sentiments of his scholars, where an arbitrary dictator, even though a wise one, could do nothing. In this, as in most other respects, a fairly large school is better off than a small one. In school, as everywhere else, where there is order to maintain, there will be a dividing line somewhere separating the orderly from the disorderly; the only danger is that this line shall separate the teacher from his class. To retain the majority on his side he need not flinch, however, from a firm administration: not even beasts of burden, much less men and boys, respect a slack rein. While firm, he must, at the same time, be also generous and magnanimous; firmness commands respect, generosity wins all but the deadest and dullest to loyalty and honour. It is the immaturity and consequent incoherence of the youthful judgment that makes the treatment of the young so difficult. In a man, there is some chance that reason will have produced some sort of unity and solidarity in his judgments and maxims; but the mind of a boy is like a kaleidoscope, rarely balanced and apt to take on suddenly an entirely new and unaccountable phase; for his feelings are strong and blind, his ideas disjointed and one-sided. Boys in this way are comparable to savages—some people say indeed they *are* savages—and certainly it is scientifically a very orthodox doctrine just now. With great activity, lively emotions, an absurdly exaggerated sense, sometimes, of their own dignity and importance, a wonderful cunning side by side with childish simplicity, they will do the most dastardly deeds without shame, and yet prepare to die rather than infringe some quixotic code of honour. In fact, just as a lamb's body seems all legs and a puppy's all head, so a boy's mind is similarly out of proportion, and may strike one sometimes as ugly and forbidding. Yet the schoolmaster must sympathize with it, as the missionary does with the natives of Timbuctoo, if any good is to be done. Schoolboys' minds are accessible from two sides; you may gain their affection when you cannot influence their judgment, and you may influence their judgment indirectly by means of the public feeling of the school, when it is amenable to no direct appeals of your own. On the principle that two heads are better than one, the collective wisdom of the school, although only childish wisdom at the best, will probably be juster, more reasonable and dispassionate than that of an individual, where an individual only is directly concerned. When the passions of all are excited, numbers doubtless do anything but multiply wisdom. Yet, if he avoid harshness, favouritism, and caprice the teacher has little reason to fear general insubordination. At the same time, since a public opinion of some sort must exist, and must tell very largely on the moral character of the school, must be either for or against his own influence, it is plain that the teacher ought to study the young and seek to influence them socially as well as individually. With the individual pupil, that treatment which is best for the pupil himself will also do most to establish the teacher's influence. The difficulty, as I have been all along trying to express, is the odd and puzzling mixture of good and bad we meet with; and, without care, it is only too possible to do a lifelong injury in correcting a childish fault. Above everything, the educator should be passionately and eagerly concerned to preserve and increase his pupils' self-respect and all the feelings that relate thereto. This is his moral life-blood, and ridicule, crushing satire, indifference, distrust and all uncharitableness will make havoc of it. In all cases of discipline, therefore, unless the culprit's conscience is against him there is little moral gain to him, whatever there may be to the school. But a tender, unpharisaic treatment of one who can be brought to condemn himself will give him new strength when he most needs it, and win good will for a teacher whose gentle fidelity rather fans than quenches the smoking flax.

And, whether discipline is in question or not, the teacher must be one with his pupils, yet ever above them. He must never allow himself to treat them as he may the men with whom he comes in contact, avoiding those he dislikes, cultivating those with whom he can sympathize, and personally resenting detraction and injustice without more ado. In this respect, too, the discipline of the school differs from the law of the land. The one is simply for protection and security, the other for correction and education. As the physician strives with equal patience to cure all, whatever

be their character, so the schoolmaster must be also no respecter
of persons. But, at the same time, and this it is which makes his
post so difficult and delicate, he must have an eye for, and an
interest in, the individuality of each one. Nothing short of an
enthusiasm like Pestalozzi's, or a sense of duty like Arnold's, will
suffice to maintain one in this position. Yet, in proportion as it
is maintained does the schoolmaster become the schoolboys' hero
—at once loved and revered. And that is after all no mean reward
which the good and faithful teacher secures; although it is a
reward that has no attraction to the selfish, it is one that those
of a generous mould can feel.

LECTURE XII

THE MORAL EDUCATION OF THE YOUNG

What we may perhaps agree to call the 'new thought' seems in some respects at a disadvantage compared with the old as regards the question of moral education: in other respects again it has an unmistakable advantage. Let us look first at the advantage. I refer to the abandonment of the doctrines of original sin or innate depravity and the doctrine of a mysterious selection of some for supernatural regeneration. In place of these we have the doctrines of heredity and natural development. On the darkest side of those old dogmas we do not need to dwell; we need not call to mind the appalling mischief they wrought alike in the heirs of grace, presumptuous antinomians, and in despairing reprobates, preordained to be children of wrath. Modern Christianity is fast outgrowing the harsh and narrow teaching of Augustine and Calvin, and is abandoning an orthodoxy—ironically calling itself evangelical—for heresies far more deserving the name of gospel. But, in spite of this, views that have been held so long and so widely are still apt—perhaps unconsciously—to exert a baneful influence on moral discipline. The parent or teacher, under this bias, is disposed to regard some trivial fault as evidence of an evil and unregenerate nature; and, perhaps, not merely to punish with undue severity, but to stigmatize as 'wicked,' acts of untruthfulness, or petty theft, or sudden bursts of temper, that are in fact the inevitable blunders of a novice, and have, it may be, no tinge of criminal intent whatever. The child, too, in the regular course of religious instruction, or from the sermon in church, or possibly from the hymns it is expected to repeat, comes more or less to identify itself with the wicked and sinful, with whom God is angry every day and whose final doom is unspeakably terrible. The result in any case is morally hurtful, though in what precise way it affects the child depends upon its temperament and disposition. I once heard of a headmaster before whom some incorrigible young offender had been summoned. The boy entered with a tearful and anxious expression. "Robinson!" the headmaster began solemnly, "any punishments that I can inflict seem useless: you are evidently going the shortest way to hell." To the master's astonishment, the boy looked at once immensely relieved. In this instance, the doctrine of juvenile depravity had had a 'hardening' effect, as the phrase is: in the case of better natures it is more likely to dishearten and depress. Most frequently it does both: diminishes moral sensibility and prevents moral enthusiasm.

One great secret of success is success itself. I have often had occasion to say to teachers: Never allow your pupils to suffer serious defeat, if only because such defeat demoralizes. But if so, then to be told that you have failed before even you have well begun to try, to feel that perhaps *you* are foredoomed to failure, can scarcely brace to ardent or hopeful enterprise. Yet this is not all. Equally disastrous are the confusing and inconsistent ideas of the moral world that must necessarily spring from a moral sense continually confronted with contradictions and unceasingly perplexed. For there is no proportion, no uniformity, no gradual advance in such a world; at the same time, there is little to hope for and everything to fear. As regards intelligence, the standard of the man is never applied to the child; but, as regards conduct, the same standard is applied again and again, though it may be thoughtlessly and in haste. If the biographies of many who grew up under what are called evangelical influences could be put in evidence I am certain it would be found that scores of the most sensitive natures have suffered, before their teens, compunction and remorse such as might reasonably be looked for after a long life of profligate and heartless villainy. In this way, conscience prematurely expends its strength over childish peccadilloes, and a violent reaction is the natural and not unfrequent sequel. There is evil enough in the world—in all truth—without our assuming that the very worst form of it, an evil will, is incarnate in our children from their birth. As they grow in years, they will fail, no doubt, of that perfection which is the ideal of our race, fail of it in character and conduct as well as in knowledge and power. But they are likely to attain to a sturdier, sounder and healthier moral type, if left to feel innocent as long and as far as they are innocent; if each particular fault is dealt with singly according to its positive demerits, and as retrievable like other failures by future success, if finally the lower pleasures honestly receive their due instead of being depreciated by a miserable asceticism, which, if we could trace things to their depths, we might find to have sprung from the tardy penitence of certain eastern debauchees. We owe to Rousseau the first vigorous protest against a pedagogy that begins with the fall and teaches the elements of morality through the dogmas of the catechism;

but, happily for us, we can urge more formidable arguments against so preposterous a method than we should find in Rousseau's *Émile*.

But in one respect, as I have said, the teacher who holds what is sometimes called the naturalistic view appears at a disadvantage, compared with the teacher who has not broken with the old dogmas. The one always regards conscience as something fundamental, the other very frequently does not. Two of the best known writers on Education, for example, Bain and Herbert Spencer, never so much as mention conscience, although they discuss the subject of moral training at some length. There are three obvious reasons for this which at once occur to me: in the first place, a reaction from that blending of the moral and religious catechism, against which we find Kant, the moralist to whom conscience was everything, protesting in language that Bain can only repeat; in the second place, the acceptance of a utilitarian basis for ethics, a basis that seems to furnish a reason for duty where intuitive morality has only a behest; and, in the third place, the more or less probable explanation of the origin and development of moral sentiments which modern psychology has achieved—an explanation that has had the effect of demeaning conscience in the eyes of many, much as Darwin's doctrines concerning the descent of man have seemed to the same minds to demean humanity, robbing it of its essential dignity and honour. All this is, I believe, but a passing phase of thought, and our own generation may quite well see the end of it. An encouraging parallel in this respect is to be drawn from the rise and rapid decline of the biological materialism that took Europe by storm about half a century ago. Still, for the present, in spite of its frequent refutation, the line of thought just described does certainly stand in the way of practical morality. Elementary schoolmasters, teaching under a 'conscience clause,' often profess themselves at a loss, falsely assuming that where religious sanctions may not be referred to, there is no ground for appealing to conscience simply. The truth is that reason which makes man capable of morality makes him also capable of religion; but of the two it is morality that is logically the more fundamental and independent. It would ill become me to state this so confidently and unreservedly, were it not a point on which the great bulk of theologians and moralists are agreed. In fact, the Christian apologist finds in moral arguments the most cogent support of his creed; and it seems plain that religion cannot at once establish morality and morality establish religion. "He that loveth not his brother whom he hath seen, how can he love God whom he hath not seen?" The merging of moral in religious sanctions, that now puts the mere moralist at a needless disadvantage, is to be accounted for in part historically. During the Christian era, the Church has been the only popular exponent of morality; but further the penalties which the Church could denounce, although their actual effect was anything but moral, were so vastly efficacious and captivating that a free and independent morality, indispensable though it was to a sincere and reasonable piety, was yet neglected and ignored. The teacher, then, who has no theological misgivings, will still do well to heed Kant's warning—"not to mix up or amalgamate the religious with the moral catechism; and above all not to suffer the former to precede the latter; for otherwise nothing but hypocrisy will come of religion afterwards—duties acknowledged out of fear, and a pretence of earnestness which is at heart a lie[1]." As to the teacher who has to let theology and religion alone, he too will do well to address himself confidently to the moral nature of the young. For though there are moral imbeciles—as there are intellectual imbeciles, or deaf-mutes, or colour-blind, or persons in other ways defective—still the existence of conscience and moral sentiments and impulses in the average child is a fact as much beyond question as its possession of five senses and general intelligence. We cannot say that it is born moral any more than we can say that it is born self-conscious and prepared for social converse; but it advances as surely and as naturally to a sense of moral obligation as it advances to a sense of its own personality; and it adopts the current moral maxims almost as instinctively as it appropriates its mother tongue. We are thus brought to the second of the difficulties I have mentioned.

How can we say: Act thus and thus, because it is right, because your conscience so bids, if we know that the real reason for such action is to be found in its utility and that, were it not thus happiness-producing or "felicific," to use Bentham's phrase, its rightness would at once be questioned and would eventually cease? The question is not wanting in subtlety, and has doubtless troubled many who would have felt in consequence a certain insincerity, as if guilty of pious fraud, in appealing to conscience as the intuitive moralist would do. And yet why not; if the utility of such a procedure is obvious, is it not *ex hypothesi* then and there right?

[1] Kant, *Jugendlehre*, Werke (ed. Hartenstein), vii, p. 296.

However, I do not for a moment imagine the difficulty is to be disposed of on any such short and easy method as that. It is, I think, unfortunate that we have got into the way of speaking of a utilitarian and an intuitional ethics, as if the two were coordinate and complete as theories and the one incompatible with the other. They are nothing of the kind: they start, so to say, from opposite ends; and, though they partly overlap, each has a department peculiarly its own. Moreover both these special departments are necessary to make the science of morals even formally complete. As in order to live, we need vitality as well as organs; as in order to manufacture, we need prime movers as well as machines, so in order to attain moral being and doing, we must have goodness as well as wisdom, a right disposition as well as sound knowledge. Now, intuitive ethics concerns itself primarily with the first or motive side of conduct, utilitarian ethics primarily with the second or executive and directive side. The world has often been injured by acts of heroic virtue, and—though it sounds satirical to say anything so trite—there are many who can demonstrate and admire plans for blessing thousands who never falter in pursuit of the happiness of one. But there is a large part of conduct, where— if he has the will—the plainest man can never fail of the way, when the balancing of consequences, the hedonic calculus or casuistical discussions are superfluities never to be thought of. This is the common ground of the intuitivist and the utilitarian; but the one has to acquire it before the other can arrange it. As speech precedes grammar, so common-sense morality precedes the utilitarian's proof of it, and it is not till he has deduced the maxims of common-sense from his greatest happiness principle that the utilitarian can proceed with any confidence to amend these in detail and extend them to new cases. We need, therefore, somewhat to modify the analogy used a moment ago; for though all the motive power is to be found in the morality of conscience, the direction and guidance is not confined to the morality that weighs consequences. This has after all both in order of time and in order of importance, quite a secondary place: it makes the common-sense moralist intellectually a moral expert. It subserves moral efforts much as instruments subserve the unaided hand or eye, which for most purposes are best unaided and must always be exercised by themselves at first. To act thus and thus because conscience so bids is always the real *moral* reason, and only conduct so determined has any moral worth or rightness: the utility of the act is only the mark that leads the judicious man to select that act as appropriate to give his intentions effect. So regarded, it can only be called right in the sense of being fit, and when, under changed circumstances, other acts are appropriate, its fitness will cease. Yet, as we know, there is a very wide field of action into which no such changes enter, and where there is a permanent coincidence between right motives and the overt acts that are their fit expression. Here it is that morality is intuitive: no sooner have we the good will to do right than we see what it is right to do. It is this good will, this zeal to do right when the right is clear, and to find it, if possible, when it is not, that is the one indispensable thing in moral character. To suppose that this can be produced, by training, from the utilitarian end is more unnatural than to suppose that a tree can begin by having branches and end by having a trunk and roots. And so we may pass to the third difficulty.

This root of the matter within, this fountain of moral life—which, for brevity, we have spoken of as conscience—what is it after all but a development out of non-moral elements—gregarious habits, family instincts, fear of authority, the impartial observation of the conduct of others and reflexion on the conduct of self, etc., etc.? Cut paste how you will, you cannot make a diamond of it, and no alloy of the baser metals will yield pure gold. You call it humanity on the outside, but 'the ape and tiger' must be all the while beneath. That very inaccurate and inapposite phrase 'mental chemistry,' which we owe to the chief expounder of utilitarianism, has, I daresay, done much to confirm such analogies: none the less I venture to think they are false entirely. A living thing is not compounded of what it has developed from. Furthermore, Shakespeare and Newton would still only have been Shakespeare and Newton, had they been created in the full maturity of their powers and never been puling infants and whining schoolboys. But where there is growth and development, there is always the possibility of progress; without these there can be none. Biology and psychology shew that advance is part of the idea of humanity, and such advance of necessity implies the evolution of higher powers out of lower ones. Morality implies self-consciousness and reason; and, therefore, cannot appear—either in the individual or in the race—till that stage of mental advance is attained. If its authority and dignity are to be impugned on this score, then all knowledge above that of sentient particulars must be surrendered too. It is certain that apes and infants have as little of logic and mathematics as they have of morality; and I think we may say psychology does not offer us an analysis of the growth of these essential constituents of science less complete than that by which it is supposed to have undermined 'the eternal supremacy of conscience.'

This familiar phrase suggests the remark that any reference to time or eternity in this connexion is apt to be ambiguous, and so misleading. All truth is eternal: time does not qualify truth but only existence. Many things are true to which there is now no answering fact and, perhaps, may never be. To take the simplest instance: it was, and is, and always will be, true that the ratio of the circumference to the diameter of a circle is a number 3·14159... which has no end, though of course no one has ever calculated the number or ever will; and it is true, though there never was a veritable circle in existence and never will be. It is true, always was and always will be true, that in a society of rational agents, in a realm of ends, to use Kant's phrase, certain principles of conduct are good and right and certain others evil and wrong. This necessary truth does not become merely contingent because the possibility of its realization or exemplification turns upon what is temporal and historical. Of all that happens, there is a sense in which we can rightly suppose it might have happened otherwise. The existence of Y is contingent on the existence of X, its cause; but X is in like manner contingent on the preceding conditions V, and so on. Yet, if Y does exist, there are certain propositions eternally and necessary true of it. If it is a plane triangle, for example, its three angles must be equal to two right angles: if it is a rational agent in a society it must have duties to others and to itself. We can perfectly well suppose that there might have been no human race at all; and it is both certain and obvious that but for certain pre-existing contingencies there *would* have been no human race. But, given the human race, then those truths of reason that are outside time of necessity apply. Man must be logical or fall into error; he must be moral or fail of his end. Like all the modes of existence that we can understand, each individual man and the whole race of men are amenable to a law of continuity: each has its growth, each has its phases. We have passed out of the darkness in which the brute only feels what is gross and palpable. We have the full light of reason about us, but we did not make it by entering into it and we are absolutely powerless to alter it, if we would. By looking back we can trace—as matter of natural history—the several stages of our way, but we cannot so explain the laws of thought or action, by which alone we can now exist as both rational and free.

To sum up, then, briefly these generalities. I have tried to shew that, as regards moral education, the new thought starts with at least one real advantage and possibly one seeming disadvantage as compared with the old. It does not assume that children start with a nature tainted either with the curse or the sin of Adam, but it is apt not to appreciate or to apply all that is involved in their having a moral nature. The gain from casting off the old tenet of original sin is a gain in brightness and hopefulness both for teacher and taught. A great cloud is lifted from off the young mind, which is free to blossom into a staunch and cheery goodfellowship. Instead of thinking to whip the wickedness out of the child, its elders may set about the easier and happier task of evoking the good that is in it; patient because they know that growth must be gradual in goodness as it is in stature, and that both may be counted on where appropriate nurture and exercise are wisely given. As to the loss that ensues from certain temporary confusions into which the new thought seems to have fallen, this can only be compensated by clearing up the confusions themselves. One can but hope that reflexion may at length assure us of three things: first, that though morality and religion have been long historically 'amalgamated,' conscience is independent of religion and religion impossible without it; secondly, that the morality of motives is in like manner prior to and more fundamental than the morality of consequences and expedients, that conscience and moral sentiments are the sole springs of rightness, while the utilitarian calculus does but shew in doubtful cases along what channels the stream of goodness can most fitly flow and furnish a criterion of such fitness applicable to all acts alike—their tendency to promote the general weal; thirdly, that moral principles like logical or mathematical principles are in themselves 'eternal and immutable,' and none the less so because human beings individually and collectively have to pass through a non-rational, non-moral stage before these principles can be consciously apprehended and obeyed. It ought to be our glory, and not our shame, that Nature, having brought us thus far, we are now as self-conscious and free agents able to work for our own perfection and for the happiness of our race. If this be truly the standpoint of modern thought, it is, it seems to me, one from which we can hopefully consider the moral education of the young.

LECTURE XIII

INDIVIDUALITY

Etymologically the words an 'atom' and an 'individual' have the same signification, yet the things signified differ profoundly, for the one belongs to the lifeless, the other to the living world. A reference to this difference may serve to introduce the topic of the present lecture. The atom is ingenerable, unalterable, indestructible; the individual is born and lives and dies. The kinds of atoms are fixed and permanent, and within each kind there is no diversity: the kinds of individuals are ever changing and within each kind there are innumerable varieties. Heredity shapes the new organism to imitate that of its parents, but the principle of variation invents for it and invests it with an individuality of its own. In the lifeless world the atom—that does nothing and suffers nothing—has no individuality; here the absence of all differences precludes even identity; in the living world the individual may attain to the dignity of a proper name. Individuality, then, presupposes variation, which is the exclusive peculiarity of living things, and among them is more pronounced and more important the higher in the scale of life we ascend. To the accumulation of such variations is to be traced all the wonderful and bewildering diversity among living forms that now meets us on every hand.

Nevertheless, on looking closer at this living world, a striking difference is at once apparent within it. Some existing forms of life—such as the Nautilus or the Lamp-shell—so-called 'persistent types,' have remained practically unaltered almost from the beginning of the geological record (that is to say, during a period reckoned in millions of years), while others—such as the horse and the dog, for example—have progressed remarkably within a time that is by comparison recent. We might be tempted to suppose that, in the first case, what I have called the imitative principle of heredity was alone operative; and that, only in the second, was the inventive principle or principle of individuality present as well. But more probably individual variations would occur in both cases —in the persistent as well as in the progressive types; but whereas in the one case some variations would be 'selected' and accumulated in the struggle for existence, in the other all would be suppressed. This difference becomes explicable when we observe that, on the one hand, the stationary types are confined to a simple and uniform environment, complete adjustment to which is easily attained—as is the case with internal parasites, for example—and that, on the other hand, progressive types are in touch with a wider and more complex environment, and one that extends as they advance. Some forms of life, in short, have drifted sooner or later into an environmental *cul de sac*: others still expatiate unrestrained.

Now, when we turn to human societies we meet again with the same contrast: some societies are stationary, some are progressive. Among the former, we find savage people still as backward as the primeval men of the Stone Age, and we find others as advanced as the Chinese, that have nevertheless remained stationary for thousands of years. In social evolution we have again two factors just as we had in biological evolution, a conservative factor—imitation in the literal sense, the analogue of heredity—and a progressive factor—individuality—the source of invention and the analogue of variation. Once more, among human societies, it is the society itself that suppresses variations, if it is stationary, doing, that is, for itself, what natural selection does for a stationary species; and it is the society itself that encourages variations and accumulates those that are fit, if it is progressive, as Nature does in the analogous case of progressive species. And for like reasons: in a stationary society variation usually means disintegration, though, while progress lasts, variations are opportunities for development. Since premature arrest of development turns out to be the rule, so that only here and there a nation escapes this untimely stagnation, we are led to ask to which of the two factors essentially concerned in nation-making such cessation of growth is due, and we are further led to wonder whether—perhaps to fear that—this common calamity of nations may yet overtake our own.

No doubt many a society has gone to pieces from overmuch variation: a nation like an individual may be too clever by half, lacking stability; but excess of individuality never yet produced the staleness and immobility of a cycle of Cathay. This danger lies wholly in the other factor of social organization, namely, imitation. And yet, without the preponderance of this factor, society would never have begun; at first, individuality would only be a hindrance. Save for his superlative gift of aping his fellows, primitive man, wild, wayward, and bird-witted, might ever have remained a solitary and intractable denizen of the woods. Even language, another condition of society, presupposes imitation. The old notion of language and government as originating in deliberate convention and contract, though long maintained by distinguished authorities, at ònce strikes the modern historical sense as false: it takes for granted the very thing it professes to explain. Aristotle's 'political *animal*' is really an absurdity; and, as to 'social contract,' that is only found where civilization has well begun. Government and language were not deliberately adopted but slowly evolved. Law, where it exists, is the outcome of custom, and custom is but imitation prolonged. Given time and repetitions enough and the custom will come and be 'a second nature.' But to secure these is just the difficulty. A group of youngsters playing 'follow the leader' is probably a true though trivial illustration of a nascent social organism. It is hard to keep the game going; but if this can be done, you may presently be confronted by a disciplined gang— hooligans or larrikins, perhaps—very difficult to disperse. To secure continuity in an infant society a strong government is, then, the first thing; if it is also a good government, so much the better, but strong it must be. Implicit obedience, a conservative, un- questioning spirit will be virtues: all originality and self-assertion on the part of the many will be treason. Those who will not follow the lead risk expulsion, perhaps extermination. For fixity of custom must be attained at any cost; amelioration may come later, if happily the customs are sufficiently plastic; but even such growth implies continuity, if not fixity, of custom,—implies, that is to say, that the conservative or imitative factor shall still be in effective operation, the new growing out of the old.

Imitation is, then, good, since society could not have originated and cannot continue without it. So much, I trust, is clear; but that imitation is likely in most cases to entail evil before long is also obvious. Through it men are tamed and taught at first, but it is liable to enslave and blindfold them afterwards: it promotes social stability and discipline at the outset, in the end it is apt to beget social stagnation and bigotry. Such, unless counteracted, are indeed the inevitable results of repetition and association. No psychological principle is surer than this. The child, open-minded, inquisitive and original, becomes a man hide-bound with pre- judice, a mere 'bundle of habits,' when only his propensity to imitation is encouraged and all his latent individuality crushed. Under such conditions most men are born and live: evidences of this most depressing truth lie about us on every hand. Historians and travellers furnish us with proofs innumerable. Only by the sacrifice of the individuality of the many has society got under way, only by subjection to what Bagehot has called "the most terrible tyranny ever known among men—the authority of 'customary law.'" "Custom is the queen of the world:

> *we draw*
> *Our right from* custom: custom *is a law*
> *As high as heaven, as wide as sea or land*."

Time would fail me, were I to attempt to recall the long roll of discoverers persecuted, reformers exiled, prophets slain at her bidding. I will content myself instead with citing an apparently trivial instance, which is nevertheless all the more impressive as showing the tendency of custom "to rule everyone in almost every action with an inflexible grasp." It is a quotation given by Bagehot in his *Physics and Politics* and refers to the Fiji Islanders. "These people," says Captain Palmer, "are very conservative. A chief was one day going over a mountain path followed by a long string of his people, when he happened to stumble and fall; all the rest of the people immediately did the same except one man, who was at once set upon by the rest to know whether he considered himself better than the chief[1]." We smile at the absurdity of such a ludicrous state of things. But would any lady nowadays venture abroad wearing a crinoline or a coal-scuttle bonnet? Yet there was a time when our revered grandmothers never ventured out without them! How horrid, say you: how becoming, said they.

The well-known psychological facts, grouped under the name of hypnotism, serve to set this situation in a true and striking light. All of you have heard of mesmeric *séances*, and many of you, I dare say, have attended them. Give a hypnotized subject a glass of vinegar with the remark, "Here's a glass of good sherry for you," and he will drink it off with gusto: give him a glass of sherry and say, "This medicine is decidedly nasty, but you must take it, for it will do you good," and he will swallow it with a wry face and unmistakable abhorrence. Now, custom is not only a despot: she is a Circe and holds her subjects under a spell. They resemble the subjects of hypnotic trance; so far as they are under her yoke, so far is their individuality suspended. They regard as beautiful and true and good whatever she proclaims as such: seeing they see not,

[1] Walter Bagehot, *Physics and Politics*, 1872, pp. 213–4.

and hearing they hear not, neither do they understand, but ruthlessly persecute and crucify the very saviours of mankind.

A few fortunate nations, however, have, as we know, succeeded so far in progressing in spite of the shackles and the spells of custom. The causes of such progress were doubtless many and complex, but the one already indicated was assuredly the chief. The individuality of the enslaved and spell-bound awakened and asserted itself, but always after a mortal struggle; and, proportionate to the success and completeness of the struggle, has been the progress that ensued. Under the ancient *régime* of custom, the place of the individual in society was fixed by the caste into which he was born; under the new *régime* of liberty, he is free to rise as high as his abilities and character will let him. Important beyond all has been freedom of thought and its expression: in all progressive countries there is incessant discussion. The foundations of the most venerable institutions, political or social, of the most consecrated beliefs, religious or moral, are laid bare, and only those that rest on the one sure bed-rock of truth can stand. Servile imitation is replaced by daring invention, arrant dogmatism by searching criticism, fanatical bigotry by large-minded toleration. New ideas are, then, the main-spring of progress; and, therefore, that people will progress the most which succeeds best in promoting and encouraging individual development, whence alone new ideas can come.

And what an advance in this respect the last century has seen! In this country, when the century began, education was withheld from the masses—save in Scotland—lest they should grow discontented with labour, and the few who were taught to read and write in charity schools were provided with a distinctive dress to remind them of their rank. From the higher education women were everywhere debarred, lest they should cease gently to acquiesce in the subjection they had so long endured. Dissenters were shut out of the old universities, lest the spread of their opinions should endanger both Church and State. Before the century closed these iniquities were in the main righted and of course without disaster: justice has never yet made the skies to fall. The masses have become more of a power and less of a danger; the intellectual emancipation of women has added to their dignity and influence; the nationalization of the universities has brought not national schism, but only national strength. Still, great as has been our educational progress, two nations at least have completely outstripped us, and no wonder, since they began two centuries earlier. I refer, of course, to Germany and the United States. As far back as 1649 the General Synod of Würtemberg made school attendance compulsory, and in 1647 the State of Massachusetts passed a law which is described as "the type of all later educational legislation throughout the United States." "It is impossible," said Horace Mann, "for us to conceive the boldness of this measure, which aimed at universal education through the establishment of free schools....But time has ratified its soundness. Two centuries of successful operation now proclaim it to be as wise as it was courageous, and as beneficent as it was disinterested." I need hardly remind you that this was the work of men of strong individuality. The mother country had said to them, parodying the Winchester motto, *aut disce aut discede*, either imitate or emigrate. They took her at her word; and, embarking in the 'Mayflower,' founded the most progressive nation the world has so far known. In Prussia education from top to bottom was nationalized with a thoroughness and efficiency that we have not even yet attained, and again by men of strong individuality who were not afraid of 'new ideas'—men such as Stein, Humboldt, Fichte and Schleiermacher. It was the hour of Prussia's humiliation, the iron heel of Napoleon was upon her and the short-sighted monarch who, not long before, had dismissed Stein from his councils was glad now to leave him and other men of ideas to regenerate the state. It was then—by the way—that Scharnhorst, who was one of them, remodelled the army from top to toe, thereby contributing quite as much as Wellington to bring Napoleon's mad career to an end, besides providing Germany with the finest military system the world has yet seen. But with us the battle of Waterloo was not preceded by the sharp lessons of adversity; and, after Wellington's declaration that it had been won on the playing fields of Eton, it is not surprising to find our Parliament in 1820 rejecting, for the second time, a scheme of national education and doing practically nothing for education of any sort for another fifty years. Should the battle of Dorking become a fact of history, perhaps the commander-in-chief may declare that it was lost in the class-rooms of Eton and similar endowed boarding-establishments, where uncultured athletes are taught everything except how to think.

During all this time we were wont to smile complacently on the so-called Spreadeagleism of the 'cute Yankee' waving his star-spangled banner, and to smile contemptuously on the so-called 'idealism' of the dreamy German, evolving camels out of his own inner consciousness. But these people, who had the start of us in respect for ideas at the beginning of the century, had more than caught us up in the practical arts before its close. And now the one is buying up our shipping, and both are fast depriving us of our old supremacy in the markets of the world, with the result that our former complacency or contempt has changed into something very like consternation. Our rivals owe their success, however, not to the possession of better leaders of men, but to the possession of better men to lead. "As in diplomacy and war, so in science," said Professor Dewar in his Address to the British Association, "we owe our reputation and no small part of our prosperity to exceptional men; and that we do not enjoy these things in fuller measure, we owe to our lack of an army of well-trained ordinary men capable of utilizing their ideas.... The root of the mischief... is in the want of education among the so-called educated classes, and secondarily among the workmen on whom these depend. It is in the abundance of men of ordinary plodding ability, thoroughly trained and methodically directed, that Germany at present has so commanding an advantage. It is the failure of our schools to turn out, and of our manufacturers to demand, men of this kind which explains our loss of some valuable industries and our precarious hold upon others. Let no one imagine for a moment that this deficiency can be remedied by any amount of that technical training which is now the fashionable nostrum. It is an excellent thing, no doubt, but it must rest upon a foundation of general training. Mental habits are formed for good or evil long before men go to the technical schools. We have to begin at the beginning, we have to train the population from the first to think correctly and logically, to deal at first hand with facts, and to evolve, each one for himself, the solution of a problem put before him, instead of learning by rote the solution given by somebody else."

This you may say truly is a counsel of perfection, an altogether impracticable ideal. Yet, are not all ideals worthy the name impracticable in the sense of being beyond immediate and complete attainment? As George Herbert has quaintly said,

> *Who aimeth at a star shoots higher far*
> *Than he who only means a tree.*

What Professor Dewar maintains is that it is not enough to make the man a better mechanic: we must make the mechanic and his

master, too, a better man. Not industrial drill but intellectual
development must be our aim, not useful information, passively
acquired, but vigorous and independent judgment—in a word, not
knowledge merely but understanding, or—in the language we have
been using—not imitation but individuality. I will ask you presently to consider the consequences of this conception of education
so far as it affects university lecturers and university students.
But let me refer for a moment to a puzzling question which the
unfavourable comparison of Great Britain with other countries
naturally suggests.

How has it come about, we ask, that the people who were
the first to achieve political and religious freedom, liberty of
the press and of private judgment, the people long pre-eminent
in industrial invention and colonial enterprise, the people, in
short, conspicuous beyond others for originality and individuality,
were among the last to nationalize education? I answer, somewhat paradoxically: largely because their very strength proved
a weakness. It was the intense individualism of the English mind
that frustrated all attempts to nationalize education for the first
seventy years of the last century. But for this, the caste and conservative arguments, to which I just now referred, would have been
unavailing; in fact, to our credit it must be said that—as against
primary education at any rate—these had long ceased to tell.
Individualism is a political creed only possible among a people
distinguished by much individuality and force of character, con-
fident that each can look after his own welfare better than the
government can, and persuaded that the untrammelled pursuit of
private interests will best promote the public welfare. Individualism seeks, therefore, to restrict the sphere of government to the
merely negative function of protecting the liberty of the individual
from the vexatious interference of others. It rejects the notion of
so-called 'paternal government,' as but a survival of the old superstition of the divine right of kings. Self-help, it maintains, is the
best form of help, the only help that makes a man self-reliant and
leaves him free. Paternal government must, therefore, ever tend to
become despotic government, not only by increasing the power and
influence of the State, but also by diminishing the individual's
energy and independence. Again, in a free country, men's convictions and tastes differ; and, so long as they provide for themselves, each may get what he wants; but, when the State provides, all
must take what they can get and none perhaps be wholly satisfied.

Think of the 'religious difficulty,' for example. According to individualism, in short, that extension of government interference and control which Socialism advocates must—even at the best—involve serious danger, not only to individual liberty, but also to that individual variety on which social progress primarily and ultimately depends. The truth of this position seems undeniable. Nevertheless, the *laissez faire* theory of individualism is now by common consent abandoned as too narrow: the State is called upon not merely to secure the liberty of the individual against infringement, but also actively to promote the general welfare of its citizens. When the many govern, it is only the few, it is said, that have to fear.

And this remark brings us to a new danger, the most serious that threatens individuality in the civilized world—a danger not from above but from below: I mean the unconscious tyranny of the majority. Democracy, though it levels up, also levels down: it tends to replace individual extremes by collective mediocrity. Private opinion counts for less and public opinion for more. Also independent thinking is rarer: before the ordinary man has time to make up his own mind on a new problem he finds it already plausibly solved for him in some public print. Accustomed all his life to be saved the trouble of thinking on vital questions, he either loses or—more likely—never acquires the power. Cheap books and journals cheaper still, free libraries and free lectures, have diffused through the length and breadth of the land a vast body of common-place thought and knowledge. Parliamentary and excursion trains enable everybody to travel: country-people flock into the towns and townspeople tour about the country. Probably the proportion of the population in the present day that has seen the sights of Paris is larger than the proportion that a century ago saw the sights of London. In brief, to use the words of J. S. Mill, "comparatively speaking, people now read the same things, listen to the same things, see the same things, go to the same places, have their hopes and fears directed to the same objects, have the same rights and liberties and the same means of asserting them. Great as are the differences of position which remain, they are nothing to those which have ceased. And the assimilation is still proceeding." I do not for a moment intend to imply that all these fruits of democracy are not good, but as little do I wish to conceal my belief that they have their drawback. If you doubt it, I would ask you to read de Tocqueville's *Democracy in America*, Bryce's

American Commonwealth, or Mill's *Essay on Liberty*, from which I have just quoted. The drawback is—to quote Mill once more—that "the combination of all these causes"—causes such as I have mentioned and other results of democratic progress that I have not had time to mention—"the combination of all these causes forms so great a mass of influences hostile to individuality that it is not easy to see how it can stand its ground." The danger is not that all angles—good and bad alike—are apt to be rubbed off in the constant attrition of the whirling crowd, if they should by chance appear; the danger is that they will never appear at all. The ordinary man and woman dread to be singular, dread to be just what they ought and were meant to be. "Not only in what concerns others, but in what concerns only themselves, the individual or the family," says Mill, "do not ask themselves—what do I prefer? or what would suit my character and disposition? or what would allow the best and highest in me to have fair play and enable it to grow and thrive? They ask themselves, what is suitable to my position? what is usually done by persons of my station and pecuniary circumstances? or (worse still) what is usually done by persons of a station and circumstances superior to mine? I do not mean," continues Mill, "that they choose what is customary, *in preference* to what suits their own inclination. *It does not occur to them to have any inclination except for what is customary.* Thus the mind itself is bowed to the yoke: even in what people do for pleasure, conformity is the first thing thought of; they live in crowds: they exercise choice only among things commonly done; peculiarity of taste, eccentricity of conduct are shunned equally with crimes: until by dint of not following their own nature they have no nature to follow."

The paramount importance of fostering individuality even in these days of universal freedom is, I trust, clear. It is, of course, no new doctrine. In the form of pleas for toleration, it was long ago advocated by the commanding eloquence and convincing arguments of Jeremy Taylor, John Milton, John Locke and a host of lesser men. And they did not plead in vain. "At the opening of the twentieth century," as Sir Leslie Stephen has put it, "we might plausibly congratulate ourselves upon the increase of mutual tolerance." Much as we have yet to learn, in this respect at any rate, we are still to the fore: we cannot indeed boast, but at least we may claim to be the most tolerant nation that exists, or has ever existed. But toleration, even complete toleration, is not enough. A spirit of toleration that is never exercised is but a 'fugitive and cloistered virtue.' What we want are new ideas to try our tolerance and challenge our attention, new ideas in every department of thought and life in which progress is possible, new ideas to be received without prejudice or prepossession, not denounced merely as innovations nor applauded merely as novelties. This is Nature's plan: with a single eye to progress, she takes all variations evenly on their merits, eliminating the old only when the new is better, and selecting the new only when the old is worse. Yet she does more: she takes pains to ensure that variations shall never be lacking, and more pains the higher the progress already attained.

> *The old order changeth, yielding place to new,*
> *And God fulfils himself in many ways,*
> *Lest one good custom should corrupt the world.*

And unless the golden age is, indeed, behind us, and the world on the decline, we have more reason to fear lest the old should last too long than we have to fear lest it should pass too soon. The customary assuredly can take care of itself: the one thing needful is to foster and promote the new. To neglect or retard that is the surest way to corrupt the world, transforming evolution into revolution, or worse, replacing development by degeneration and decay.

Toleration, then, is reasonably secure: the laws allow it and public opinion condemns bigotry and narrow-mindedness—especially in minorities. But that something more, something positive which we demand, the nurturing, encouraging and maturing of individuality is beyond the scope of legislation and cannot be left to chance,—that, I venture to think, is the main business of education, and especially of university education. "The business of education," said Locke, "is not...to make the young perfect in any one of the sciences, but so to open and dispose their minds as may best make them capable of any, when they shall apply themselves to it. It is, therefore, to give them this freedom that I think they should be made to look into all sorts of knowledge, and exercise their understandings in so wide a variety and stock of knowledge. But I do not propose it as a variety and stock of knowledge, but *as a variety and freedom of thinking: as an increase of the powers and activity of the mind, not as an enlargement of its possessions.*" Not mental possessions but mental power and activity; in a word, not to impart knowledge, but to draw out and develop individuality is,

I repeat, the first concern of all education, and most of all of university education. After all, the child is still at the imitative stage, and the school is a place for drill; but in a university we put away childish things. A university student is not a pupil and a university professor is not a tutor. The primary function of a university is not to diffuse knowledge but to increase it. An ideal university is a place in which men, distinguished for their originality and actively engaged in research, single out and train the most promising of the rising generation to carry on their work. In Germany—and even in Russia and Norway—this ideal is already in large measure an accomplished fact; there "the explicitly avowed aim of the higher education is to turn the student into an instrument for advancing scientific discovery." He can obtain his degree only by adding his mite to the sum of human knowledge; in what way he does this, it is left to him to choose. There is no rigidly-prescribed syllabus to hamper either professor or student: *Lehrfreiheit* and *Lernfreiheit* are alike complete. How different from the complicated examinational machinery still maintained in this country and in France, which cramps the individuality both of teachers and of learners! Things are mending, happily. The most hopeful sign of all is that at last—fifty years and more behind the rest of the world—this country, which, as an important educational official has said, had "so wastefully blundered and muddled through the long and critical century" then closing, is now about to take the step that logically comes first of all, is about to train its teachers. "Give me the training of teachers," said Bishop Percival, "and I count all other matters of secondary importance." And, assuredly, that training will fall into very bad hands if a generation hence the development of individuality is not avowed as the supreme end of intellectual education, an end to which the acquisition of knowledge is wholly secondary and subservient. Hitherto scouted as wild and visionary, though maintained by thoughtful men from Socrates' day till our own, it will, I verily believe, by that time be accepted as practical common sense.

"But we have no originality," some may say: "we are not conscious of budding wings that we might perfect by flapping: we admire the flights of genius, but should only look silly were we to try to soar." Well, I am willing—for argument's sake—to allow that you are not all geniuses, but at any rate—as a distinguished Master of Trinity once said in a College sermon—"you all have one talent, some of you have even two," and that is enough. Yet no two of us have the same talent: we may be pretty sure of that. The doctrine which the Schoolmen held concerning angels, that each one was *sui generis*, that no two were alike, is surely true of human kind. Granted, then, that you can only walk on *terra firma* and cannot mount over the heads of your fellows to cleave the upper air, still that is no reason for not striking out a path of your own, no reason for submitting for ever to leading strings and always following slavishly in the wake of a crowd. To do this is to bury your talent; and, for fear of risking anything, to lose everything, to be but like dumb driven cattle and not as heroes in the strife. A nation where many are, or have to be, content with such a *rôle* cannot be progressive.

To make this clear, I must go back a step. It is the fashion to talk of the soaring flights or the marvellous inspiration of genius. Such imagery is, however, misleading, oftener false than true. It is altogether a mistake to imagine that ordinary men can only hack their way through a thicket of difficulties which for great men disappear as by a touch from a magician's wand. As a rule, it is the man of five talents who is the hardest worker, and the men who doubt if they have one who are oftenest lazy, who are prone to lay the blame on Nature and, as Locke said, "to complain of want of parts when the fault lies in their want of improvement of them." More real humility is what such men need: they cannot set the Thames on fire, and so they hide their candle under a bushel instead of bettering the world and themselves by making the most of its light. And the result of such ineffectiveness in the many who have one talent—whether that be their fault or their misfortune—is that the few who have more talents are often doomed to failure for lack of co-operation and support. A telling instance in point is furnished by Professor Dewar in a part of his Address from which I have already quoted. I will give it in brief. "The consular report estimates the whole value of German chemical industries at not less than fifty million sterling *per annum*. ...The fundamental discoveries upon which this gigantic industry is built were made in this country and were practically developed to a certain extent by their authors. But in spite of the abundance and cheapness of the raw material—[namely, coal-tar]—and in spite of the evidence that it could be most remuneratively worked up, these men founded no school and had practically no successors. The colours they made were driven out of the field by newer and better colours made from their stuff by the development of their ideas, but these improved colours were made in Germany and not in England. Now, what is the explanation of this extraordinary and disastrous phenomenon? I give it in a word—want of education. We had the material in abundance when other nations had comparatively little. We had the capital, and we had the brains, for we originated the whole thing. But we did not possess the diffused education, without which the ideas of men of genius cannot fructify beyond the limited scope of an individual." Alas! how many times in the history of the world have the ideas of great men failed of their fruit—ideas not merely of industrial but of the highest political and social importance—and failed solely for lack of intelligence and sympathy on the part of their fellows! Such men were before their age, the times were not ripe for them, the soil was not yet prepared: such are the cold comments with which we often content ourselves, as if social movements necessarily depended on natural causes analogous to wintry frosts or spring breezes, as if individuality pertained only to the distinguished few and the rest were verily an inert mass, helpless when at rest and dangerous when in motion. So far as men cannot or at least do not think, this is a true account of them, it is false in proportion as they can think and do. Yet mere knowledge is no adequate equivalent for intelligence; for we constantly find great sagacity along with a good deal of ignorance—usually enforced ignorance—and great stupidity along with a good deal of knowledge, usually a knowledge that has been painfully 'pounded in.'

We hear much of the solidarity of modern civilization. It means for one thing that progress is only possible when the intelligence of those capable of ruling thousands is seconded by the intelligence of others, in adequate numbers, capable of ruling hundreds, of ruling fifties, of ruling tens. Collectively these lesser lights have been as important and as indispensable, though their names are unknown to fame, as the brilliant few whose dazzling achievements history has enshrined. In legislation and administration, in science, in industry and in commerce, national success depends on this orderly and continuous organization of intelligence from the highest positions down to the lowest. A wise statesman has no chance if the electors are mostly fools. Local government is impossible where there are no village Hampdens. Industrial development must halt at the line where the hands that work have not heads of their own to guide them. Even the pace of science is limited by the number of its students capable of observing and recording new facts. A nation, then, devoid of this organized intelligence is so far unformed and lifeless; its limbs are paralysed; it may have a golden head but its feet are clay. Other intellectually better organized nations may utilize the ideas of what Professor Dewar calls its 'exceptional men,' or may even carry off the men themselves—as Mr Carnegie proposes to do—but that nation has attained the stationary state and decline may soon follow. This is the danger that threatens us, a danger which we are beginning to realize. We must hope that it is not too late, but there is one ominous fact we cannot overlook. We have certainly not taken time by the forelock—that opportunity lies at least half a century behind us. So far the outlook is desperate. But, on the other hand, our national fibre has not yet lost its suppleness or its grit. There is still no people that can surpass us in the thoroughness and pertinacity with which we carry through whatever we once undertake.

Now, what the new century demands of us, I contend, is the development of individuality, and particularly the individuality of average men and women, the people who have hitherto been supposed to have no individuality at all. The mistake we have made in the past is that we have set knowledge in the first place; not educating in the strict sense, but imparting useful information. The mistake is a very natural one, most men are prone enough to admit their lack of knowledge; they are by no means so ready to admit their lack of wit. As Locke shrewdly observes: "When by their want of thought...they are led into mistake...they impute it to any error, accident, or default of others, rather than to their own want of understanding; that is what nobody discovers or complains of in himself." But their want of definite information they cannot but realize, when they see others prosper by the possession of facts and figures .of which they are themselves in ignorance, and so like simple Mr Tulliver they say: "I want my son to be even wi' them fellows as have got the start o' me with having better schooling. Not but what if the world had been left as God made it, I would ha' seen my way and held my own wi' the best of 'em." So it comes about that though what young minds especially want is training, what they get is learning. 'Knowledge is power,' no doubt, but it is power only for those who can use it.

Massage and feeding up, the so-called 'rest cure,' is a poor thing even for a body out of health, but any similar treatment of a healthy-growing mind is altogether pernicious. Knowledge that cannot be applied is useless to its possessor unless, forsooth, he can make shift to impart it—as so much dead lore—to others.

"Take exercise and your appetite will take care of itself," it is said: train the mind and the healthy assimilation of knowledge will take care of itself, is equally true. And the assimilation is healthy assimilation only when the individuality of the student is fostered to the utmost. To this end clear exposition is not the first thing, though when easy acquisition is our only aim, it is all important. In mental training two things quite distinct from this are vitally important—(1) the student's own difficulties and (2) the history of the past progress of the subject that he studies. In our hurry to impart results this last point is commonly neglected altogether. When nature builds up the embryo organism she recapitulates in its individual development all the leading stages that the race has traversed. Yet when we try to make a mathematician or a chemist, we leave all but the latest stage out of account.

But these are considerations rather for those of us who try to train: for those who seek training the one point I would urge is to invert the Baconian axiom: say not that knowledge gives power, but rather that power gives knowledge. Let them have a care that their minds grow and be not anxious about their possessions. For them *spes, non res laudanda est*: mental sinews now are the best earnest of knowledge in days to come. To be wise, not learned, is the main thing; in a word to be philosophers, or, at least, to be philosophic. Lest this should sound too extravagant, let me quote a definition of a philosopher which shews that the philosophic mind is within the reach of everybody. "The philosopher," said Faraday, "should be a man willing to listen to every suggestion, but determined to judge for himself. He should not be biassed by appearances; have no favourite hypothesis; be of no school; and in doctrine have no master. He should not be a respecter of persons, but of things. Truth should be his primary object. If to these qualities be added industry, he may hope to walk within the veil of the temple of nature." Let every student work in this spirit and the individuality that as a nation we so sorely need will assuredly not fail us.

LECTURE XIV

PERSONALITY THE FINAL AIM OF EDUCATION

Since the days of Lamarck, at the beginning of the nineteenth century, there has been among biologists a ceaseless collecting of facts and propounding of theories about heredity. Organic or physical heredity we must henceforth call it; for by the end of the century another form of heredity had become a not uncommon topic with sociologists—social or moral heredity, that is to say. By this we are to understand more than the tradition which, in a very strict sense, is the individual's social inheritance. That, however, is usually spoken of as his social environment—the legal, economic, and intellectual conditions, in a word, the civilization, of the time and place in which the individual is born. Social heredity in the narrower sense is to be distinguished from social environment, much as physical heredity is distinguished from physical environment—such circumstances, for example, as climate, food, and shelter that affect the visible organism as soon as it is born. Environment, in both cases, implies something static, a permanent situation that is common to many. Heredity in both cases suggests rather a continuous process or development, that is always more or less unique for each; the process, in fact, whereby his individuality is gradually shaped and differentiated.

The physical process comes first, and may be said to end in the bodily constitution and congenital endowments, the *natural* or inborn qualities, with which the child begins its separate life. The prime factors in this process are the germs or "gametes" which the parents contribute to form the embryo of the new individual. To realize the importance to the future of our race of heredity in this sense, we need only "to parade before our mind's eye" the rickety, misshapen inmates of our orthopædic hospitals, or the juvenile imbeciles of our lunatic asylums, or the anæmic crowds "with narrow chests and weak chins" who, if they have the means, "expatriate themselves for the chance of life" to sunnier climes; and if they have not, fall a prey to tuberculosis before they are out of their teens[1]. Facts such as these it was that led Sir Francis Galton, a cousin of Darwin's, to found and endow the movement which has led to the present Eugenics Society.

[1] Cf. Galton, *Inquiries into Human Faculty*, 1883, p. 23.

Where physical heredity ends, there social heredity begins: the one, it is commonly said, is concerned with *nature*, the other with *nurture*. Yet the earlier process sets limits to the later. "You cannot," said Henry the Eighth, "make a silk purse out of a sow's ear"; and Prospero called Caliban "a born devil, on whose nature nurture can never stick." Such incorrigibles, the morally demented, are a sociological problem to be dealt with apart: we must here leave them out of account. But even those who start with a normal human nature may degenerate and acquire characters as bad and almost as hopeless, or they may develop into honest and honourable citizens. To prevent the one and to promote the other is the function of social eugenics. As we regard physical heredity as ending when the mature embryo becomes a viable organism, so we regard social heredity as ending when the legal infant becomes in the eyes of the law a fully responsible person, a member of the commonwealth. During this period of nonage or legal immaturity the so-called "minor" is the ward of society. The prime factors in determining the sort of character or personality with which he or she will "come out" when either arrives at full age are the influences —the practices and the precepts—of those about them who educate or draw out their native possibilities. And we must remember that the possibilities for evil are more easily educable than those for good. Such social dysgenics has then to be prevented and forestalled. Omitting, however, further reference to this as mainly negative or repressive, we come in sight of what we specially mean by Social Eugenics. As the advocates of physical eugenics seek "to disseminate knowledge and encourage action in the direction of perpetuating a higher racial standard," so the advocates of social eugenics seek to spread knowledge and promote action with the view of fostering a fuller, higher, and wider civic and moral life.

This language is, however, not sufficiently precise; for the problem of social eugenics is more complex than at first sight it seems to be. Social heredity, no doubt, points clearly enough to the individual. But when we say the aim of social eugenics is to promote civic and moral life—even when we add by means of education—our aim is only partly defined. The individual may be the end, he may be only a means. In educating the young the question is: Do we intend to provide them with such nurture as will ensure that they make the very best of themselves, or such nurture as will adapt them the most to the service of the existing social whole? Even physical eugenics has before now been diverted to special ends; as, for example, that of adding to the stature of his favourite regiment by Frederick William I of Prussia, the father of Frederick the Great. To this end he was credited with selecting the tallest women he could find as wives for his famous Potsdam Guards. When we remember the variety produced among our domesticated animals by less distinguished 'fanciers,' it makes one shudder to think of what a Frederick William might make of mankind in these days if he had the chance.

Doubtless this danger is imaginary, but with social eugenics there is a real danger, if a less sensational one. There are other fables besides Mandeville's to be drawn from a beehive. All the difference between a queen bee and a worker is said to be due to difference of nurture applied to the same nature. Here is material for a new fable. I turn again to Germany for illustration. She affords us at this moment both encouragement and warning: she shews us at once how much social eugenics may hope to accomplish and at the same time how disastrous it may be if misapplied. For Germany has not neglected to make the formation of character the chief aim in school life; and the result she has attained is a demonstration of what method and singleness of purpose can do. But, on the other hand, the character she has succeeded in forming has reduced her citizens severally to so many pliant instruments of an autocratic government, instead of fitting them to act collectively as the sovereign power of a democratic one. There is happily neither the will nor the way to such an abuse of a natural trust anywhere in the British Commonwealth: that I know, of course. Yet, notwithstanding the happier political environment that after centuries of liberty we have now consolidated for ourselves, we are still at the crossways, hesitating between education in the individual's interest and the German ideal, "education to the State, and for the State, as well as by the State."

It may be said that the true interests of the Man and the State cannot conflict. Of the ideal State we certainly must allow this: we might even frame it into a definition of what a State ought to be. Or, it may be said, that what chiefly hinders the realization of this ideal is just the keen eye and the zest everybody has for his own interests, contrasted with his extreme insensibility and obtuseness to the general welfare. "*Every man for himself*—and God for us all*" is the maxim by which men live. There is no need, then, it is said, to foster egoistic interests. The young scarcely require to be trained to take care of number One: they *must* be trained to care for others. Perhaps nobody—at any rate, no thoughtful person, —would make this reply; for it rests on a complete misunderstanding. The true interests of the individual involve the fullest possible realization of his highest self, and are not to be gained by a self-suppression like the Bushido or "national spirit" of Japan. And now my point is that it is here most of all that the young need help—help which training with a view to what are assumed to be the interests of the State will not give them. Yet, before passing to this point, a remark that the supposed objection suggests is worth making. The pure altruism of the Comtist's *vivre pour autrui* is just as one-sided and, if it could be fully realized, would be perhaps just as detrimental to social progress, as pure egoism—which, after all, is equally unnatural and equally rare. For, save in the morally imbecile, some sympathy and fellow-feeling are always to be found. But indiscriminate charity or such amiable generosity as Oliver Goldsmith's—said to be the characteristic of all Irishmen—who always found something for a beggar but rarely had anything for his creditors, is neither morality nor civic virtue, and not a disposition to encourage.

Now for my point. We may agree that ideally the true interests of the Man and the State cannot conflict. When that stage of progress is reached, Herbert Spencer's famous exposition of this conflict will have only a historical interest. Meanwhile, that day is a far-off event. At present, there is anything but harmony between the truest interests of the individual and the interests of society, *as society now conceives them*. If, then, you aim at inculcating—I use this hateful word because it belongs to the terminology of the theories I oppose—if you aim, I say, at inculcating the principles of conduct that now predominate, you will certainly improve upon the German model of a citizen—which, by the way, owes its shape largely to the use of heels—but you will fall sadly short of educating to the utmost the highest possibilities of the rising race. In plainer words, the type of human being that would suffice to meet the present effective demand of society is not the highest type, is very far from it. This you may say is a very grave indictment. It is, and the position of the Civic and Moral Education League—like a voice crying in the wilderness—is a proof that it is no baseless charge. "The formation of character ought to be the chief aim in education" we say. Yet, though there has been much discussion in Parliament and in the Press about the new education after the war, this all-important topic, the foundation of the whole, has been almost completely ignored. It is agreed on all hands that the nation must make up for its shameful neglect of scientific education; not, however, from any newly awakened interest in science for its own sake, but simply because at length its technical value has been brought home to us by the Germans. To this end, then, it is proposed without hesitation or misgiving to sacrifice the *literae humaniores* and the higher studies generally; though their bearing on character and a wider, more creative life cannot be questioned. Very different, I am sure, is your conception of the most pressing demand of the times. It is not education with a view to a more efficient economic rivalry when at length hostilities have ceased —according to rivalry the motto *fas est et ab hoste doceri*. It is not military training as "the best antidote to individualism" and as a remedy against "the growth of syndicalist ideas and strikes"— I quote some recent writers. The eager race for wealth we do not regard as a pursuit to encourage; for "a man's life consisteth not in the abundance of the things that he possesseth." National defence we do regard, I take it, as a duty that a citizen cannot devolve on others; but what we strive for is the time when we may "beat our swords into ploughshares and our spears into pruning hooks." But I must pause to anticipate an interruption to this attempt to outline what I take to be our view.

It will be said, perhaps, and with some impatience, these are not practical ideals. Of course not: no ideals are practical, and none ever become so but those men strive to realize. The first thing is conviction as to the worth of an ideal: faith in its attainment then becomes possible. It ought to be, therefore it can be. Given these, all the rest—the methods, the ways and means—will then be added unto us. Put to the test of numbers such ventures of faith are always outvoted at first; but let the world remember in this connexion Ibsen's fine saying: "the minority may be right, the majority is always wrong." Let us then not be afraid of seeking or of boldly proclaiming our ideal. But, now, so far as my somewhat slight acquaintance with the literature of educational reformers extends, I find much that is most excellent as regards ways and means of progressing beyond the present situation, yet I find little to indicate the ideal end they seek.

> *I have urged you forward and still urge you—*
> *Without the slightest idea of our destination.*

So spake Walt Whitman, and so many of these seem to speak. No bad advice either, you may say, provided we have the sense to discriminate between "forward" and "backward," and so much moral sense we think we have: *ein guter Mensch in seinem dunklen Drange ist sich des rechten Weges wohl bewusst.* I agree: at the same time I think less *Drang* and more reflexion would ensure a clearer insight. The ant and the bee may both get home at last, but the bee's superior sense of direction saves it from the meanderings in which the ant often loses its way and itself into the bargain.

At no time could the demand for some clear "idea of our destination" well be more urgent than it is now. People on all hands are realizing that the old civilization is passing away; and the new social reconstruction that will replace it is being everywhere anxiously awaited. Now, as in all great epochs, ideas are in what chemists call "the nascent state"—set free from old, and ready for new, combinations. When Russia casts off her Czar and America lays aside its Monroe doctrine, visions may be hailed as inspired that but yesterday would have been hooted down as mad. For example, here in a well-known weekly paper I read: "The nation that first appreciates the ideal of Ibsen—that every child in the land should be brought up as a nobleman—will lead the world." If I were attempting that other Fable of the Bees of which I spoke, this passage and the following might point the moral: I quote now from a recent pamphlet entitled *What Labour wants from Education.* "Hitherto," says Mr M'Tavish, the writer, "the working class has never been seriously consulted as to what it wants from education. [It is expected] to fit in with preconceived notions as to its proper place in a generally accepted scheme of things; and educational reform is only to concern itself with equipping *the workers to be more efficient bees in the industrial hive.*"

We must try to realize that there will be henceforth no "generally accepted scheme of things," and that, therefore, the task of reconstructing will devolve on individuals no longer helped or hindered by vested interests. The more we realize this, the clearer the problem of social eugenics will become. When a city has to be extended, the old plan is there to prejudice the new; but when the city has to be rebuilt, the old defects survive only as a warning. The law of progress, Sir Henry Maine taught us, has been a movement from Status to Free Contract: we may enlarge this and say that it has become a movement from Status towards Free Personality. Henceforth the one thing needful is that the men and women who are fit to rebuild—that these, whatever be the class they come from, and only these, shall be promoted to the work and socially ennobled.

"The greatest spiritual tragedy of working-class life," says another W.E.A. pamphleteer, "is disclosed in the phrase, 'I never had a chance.'" Henceforth everyone is to start with the nobleman's chance: one may have it thrust upon him, but all are to have the opportunity to achieve it; and only by achieving may any hope to retain. After all, in so far as the existence of society is due to the *nature* of individuals, in so far, it seems plain, that its progress must depend on the *nurture* of those individuals. The very continuity which we now recognize between rational human nature and its animal (or anœtic) antecedents suggests this priority of the individual to the whole by which he is nevertheless to be transfigured. Only, in times like the present, when a thorough reconstruction of society is imperative, have men ever realized the full significance of this simple truth that society has been, and always will be, what its members make it. Obviously, then, the many who are now beginning to feel the force of this elementary truth must also begin to see the folly of sacrificing the means to a better state of society for the sake of a worse. That is what education in the interests of society has long meant, and what it will still mean, unless we cease talking "of making the man a better mechanic," and strive mainly and primarily to make the mechanic a better man.

To strengthen my case for the initial value of personality in social structure, I will venture yet further afield. I will ask you to imagine what the ideal society will be like—in plainer words, if you prefer them, to imagine what heaven will be like. It is doubtless a wild question. Never mind, you have some ideas; and I think I can guess certain of them. There will be no want, no struggle, therefore, for subsistence, no private property perhaps. At any rate there will be no real temptation. Everybody will be as pure as they look, overflowing with goodwill and radiant with love. But what will they *do*? Get up missions to the denizens of hell?— unless these once for all have chosen evil for their good and ceased to be. Or visit the spirits in prison perhaps, for whom all hope is not yet abandoned. This would doubtless, as Bret Harte said, be "a...better business than loafing around a throne." Yet such possibilities seem incompatible with an ideal consummation of all things, which is what we mean. What when the *whole* world is perfect will everybody do? Find delight in creation and in friendship is the only surmise we can make as to a state that wholly transcends our imagination. It was, I take it, on these lines that the scholastic doctrine grew up that every angel was *sui generis*, and interesting, therefore, to every other. Our experience, at any rate, knows of no other escape from insipidity: true personality is the salt of the earth. And a survey of animate nature points in the same direction: as Goethe said, *die Natur scheint Alles auf Individualität angelegt zu haben* ("Nature seems to have planned everything with a view to individuality"). Our surmise, then, suggests anew the supreme value—we may call it this time the final value—of personality.

But further to bring out my point, I will ask you to look at the matter in yet another way. Glancing back over the history of our race, we find one of its most striking features to be the influence of great men. The plausible but shallow attempts of writers such as Buckle, Spencer, Taine, and many more, to shew that great men, like all men, are but resultants to be explained along with other "phenomena" by their antecedents and their environment, on pain of denying the law of universal causation,—these attempts no longer impress us[1]. From the mechanical standpoint, the law of causation may hold out to the last—as there an indispensable postulate. Yet, from the standpoint of history, the last fact we reach is some great Supreme, who wrought

> *But this main miracle, that thou art thou*
> *With power on thine own act and on the world.*

I will refer, therefore, without misgiving, to such pioneers in the moral realm as, say, Confucius, Buddha, Socrates, and, above and beyond all, Jesus Christ as being pre-eminent instances of the power of personality in human affairs. Beginning with these, the principle of continuity should help us to realize that influences the same in kind have been at work from the first and are working now, though exerted in narrower and narrower spheres till we come down at length to that of the mute inglorious Miltons and village Hampdens, of whom there has been and will be no historic record. Such reflexion should, then, convince us that we shall never clearly understand history so long as we are content to talk vaguely of general tendencies, social movements, public opinion, *Zeitgeist* or the spirit of the age, and so forth. These are actual and

[1] Cf. W. James's Essay on "Great Men and their Environment," *Will to Believe*, pp. 216–54.

efficient only in so far as they are incorporated in concrete individuals: the veritable creators and conservers of the whole are not diffused forces, they are distinct persons[1].

Creators and conservers, I have said: the duality of function here implied suggests some remarks that may again help us forward. Stability is essential if society is to exist at all; for this imitation and obedience may suffice: these make up the conservative factor, answering to custom and routine. But for progress, invention and initiative are required: these constitute the creative factor, which means change and reformation. Yet, in what Bagehot has called the preliminary age, the two rôles were and had to be distinct: in what he calls the age of discussion, they are and have to be combined[2]. Or as Tarde, in his masterly work, *Les Lois de l'Imitation*, puts it: at first imitation was *unilateral*, at length it became *reciprocal*: those who led in some capacities were prepared to follow in others, and *vice versa*. Now, when we recall what ages of struggle against suppression it has taken to advance from the one extreme—essential to existence but inimical to progress —towards the other, in which progress is assured, we may be more willing to admit the common defect in educational systems against which I am trying to protest. For, towards the young, we are apt to conduct ourselves as if the world were still in the preliminary age. While we nowadays only bow, they are still expected to bow down—I suppose everybody knows of the originals, of which our modern bow and other formalities of courtesy are but the atrophied survival. Children are "to be seen not heard," "to speak when they are spoken to," "to come when they are called," "to do as they are bid without asking why," and so forth. I expect few—save the youngest among us—have escaped this *régime*: indeed, none of us can have escaped it altogether, or we should not be here. For, obviously, the parental relation is in every respect "unilateral," at the first: the child does and must begin by imitating and obeying those on whom its very existence depends. Still, in bringing up children parents, and teachers too, easily forget the potentialities of the child and the pace at which these become actualities. As the child's stature increases rapidly, so too does its experience. A decade that often extends but little the parental horizon widens enormously that of their offspring. What the biologists call palingenesis has its

---

[1] Cf. J. A. Leighton, "The Psychological Self and the Actual Personality," *Philosophical Review*, 1905, p. 678.

[2] *Physics and Politics*, chapters i and v.

analogue here. The newly hatched chicken, they tell us, acquires in three weeks the organization that the primary evolution or *élan vital*, as I suppose Bergson would call it, took untold ages to "canalize" or map out. Equally rapid is the rate at which the child enters upon its social inheritance, that tradition which reaches back into prehistoric times.

Yet this neglect both of parents and teachers to recognize adequately the early and rapidly developing personality of the young is easily explained. In the first place, they are only treating the rising generation as they were treated themselves. So the evil gets perpetuated and confirmed; partly because, when their turn comes to exercise arbitrary authority, parents and teachers have usually forgotten what they suffered under it; partly because the present sufferers are as yet helpless—only aggravating the evil if their nature impels them to resent it. In the next place, the customary routine is immediately effective; but sparing the rod means spoiling the child and risking the need of sterner remedies later on. Authority must be maintained, and the rod is its symbol. Thus it comes about that the type of government characteristic of the primitive age is upheld even now in the "management of the young." Only by sacrificing individual initiative to custom has society got under weigh, and a like sacrifice is still assumed to be needful for the young, even when we adults are living in the age of discussion. Moreover, it saves so much trouble to work with machinery and to one pattern: in fact, production on a large scale is only possible in this way. But, even if education were an art comparable—as it is so often supposed to be—to the potter's art in moulding clay, personal handling would still be vastly superior to "knocking into one shape" all and sundry to reach a prescribed "standard." The potter at his wheel at least feels his material; and, in giving it form, can take its quality into consideration: neither is possible to the potter at a press. The greater value of hand-made articles, then, might lead us to question mechanical methods of education, even if the young were merely so much plastic material that may safely be dealt with in the lump. Yet what is too much overlooked is that the young are not inertly plastic—only imitating and obeying—but spontaneously plastic— full of mischief as their elders say, but always original mischief, displaying their inborn inventiveness.

What, however, specially impresses me in the teaching of men like Bagehot and Tarde is the presumption they suggest—as I hinted just now—that when the position of the adult is altered that of the *alumnus* should be altered too. "Were slavery to be his lot," said Herbert Spencer, "if his after-life had to be passed under the rule of a Russian autocrat, or of an American cotton-planter, no better method of training could be devised than one which accustomed him to that attitude of complete subordination he would subsequently have to assume. But just to the degree in which such treatment would fit him for servitude, must it unfit him for being a free man among free men[1]." "That's enough in all conscience," some will say; and anywhere but here I might be shouted down. "In a word," they might add, "we gather you want to enfranchise children!" Yes, I do. We are in process of enfranchising women at last, and the children's turn would appear to come next. "When the child is free the world will be rebuilt," was said recently at a symposium about "The Ethical Principles of Social Reconstruction[2]." But the enfranchisement I mean is one appropriate to the special case: it is an educational enfranchise-ment, and has nothing to do with the electoral franchise. I mean the removal of every hindrance and the provision of every facility, so that freedom of thought and action may be displayed within the steadily enlarging bounds of juvenile life. The United States, many of which have anticipated us in the matter of woman suffrage, are also, I understand, greatly in advance of us here.

A powerful argument, as it seems to me, for this early enfranchise-ment of those who have soon to take up the full responsibilities of citizenship is also suggested by the bare fact of social progress itself. To what was the progress due? Ultimately simply to this—that the children were wiser than their fathers. Ancestor-worship is a widely spread and ancient cult; its true inwardness, however, is still uncertain. If we regard it as a commemoration of bene-factors, we may ask: To whom do we owe most—to the ancients or to the moderns? Well, the later Jews, we remember, were commanded to teach their children that "they might *not* be as their fathers were." And are we not constantly doing the same? It is surely probable—nay, it is our devout belief—that our children will retrieve our faults and be wiser than we have been. If, then, we honour our fathers for what they were, should we not reverence our children for what they will be? And in fact they, as has been often said, are the true ancients after all; for they will

[1] *Social Statics*, 1892, p. 85.
[2] *Proceedings of Aristotelian Society*, N.S., vol. xvii, 1917, pp. 256 *sqq.*

constitute that older, and so wiser and better, world that will have outgrown the comparatively inexperienced days to which we belong. Mr Bertrand Russell in his *Principles of Social Reconstruction* speaks of *reverence* for the child as essential to the teacher; though lacking, alas! far too often from mere thoughtlessness and want of imagination. For, adapting Tennyson's words, we may say:

> *The world which credits what is done*
> *Is cold to all that will have been.*

But if we "take wings of foresight"—as Tennyson in the next canto goes on to say—and credit what hereafter will have been done as well as what has been done already, must we not feel that honour is due to our children as well as to our parents? Looking at the world *sub specie aeternitatis*, that is *what we should do*. Personally, I confess, I have long felt that "unaccountable humility" in the presence of a child, which Mr Russell describes, whenever my thoughts have led me to think of the child's future; and never have I felt it more than in these latter days when such vast tasks are soon to await the erstwhile child, tasks in reconstructing our social systems that time has tried and proved wanting.

People in general are, however, too absorbed with the present to be duly sensible of the dignity and worth that its future entails upon the rising generation. We talk mostly of the submerged tenth of the population, but Lord Haldane, as everybody knows, has lately shewn that as regards education it is a submerged nine-tenths that we ought to talk of. Our callousness to this awful waste and injustice will some day be condemned as universally and as severely as the indifference of our forefathers to the evils of slavery is condemned now. But there is another kind of waste and injustice that would remain, even if the nine-tenths—treated more or less as chattels—received all the education the favoured tenth obtain. The education itself is bad; for it regards social eugenics as a means for which society itself, not the individual, is the end. Thereby society shews itself an *injusta noverca* rather than an *alma mater*, providing an education that tends to keep the world stationary rather than to promote its progress. And so far it is short-sighted as well as selfish.

The value of a single man or woman of open mind, independent judgment, and moral courage, who requires to be convinced and refuses to be cajoled, is only concerned to be right and not afraid to be singular, deferring to reason but not to rank, true to his or her own self, and, therefore, not false to any man—the value of such a man or woman, I say, is priceless: a nation of such would leaven and regenerate the world. That is the true national education at which England should aim. What we actually aim at is something immeasurably inferior. Great advances in national education were made, it must be allowed, in the course of the last century; and yet class interests, political jealousies, and sectarian differences blocked the way for seventy years or more. Then University Tests were abolished and Board Schools began; and since, great strides have been made, and greater still are pending. But the evil influences that formerly delayed the movement are still powerful to check its perfect work. Prejudices venerable only for their age, class interests that are morally unjustifiable, conflicting dogmas that cannot all be right and may quite well all be wrong, still bar the attainment of full liberty of thought and the complete development of each one's personality.

INDEX

For EU product safety concerns, contact us at Calle de José Abascal, 56–1°,
28003 Madrid, Spain or eugpsr@cambridge.org.

www.ingramcontent.com/pod-product-compliance
Ingram Content Group UK Ltd.
Pitfield, Milton Keynes, MK11 3LW, UK
UKHW010049140625
459647UK00012BB/1708